A Century of Excellence

No. 34 Bed Couch

Hard edge. 28 in. wide, 6 ft. 3 in. long. With mattress.
When open, width, 4 ft. 10 in.
Grade, tapestry No. 15

2228-16 Desk

No. 36—Extension Table

No. 59—Extension Table

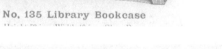

No. 135 Library Bookcase

Armchair

A Century of Excellence
Krug Bros. & Co. Furniture Manufacturers

No. 220 Morris Chair

Quarter-Sawed Oak.
Mission Style.
Loose Reversible Cushions.

Booming
New Furniture Factory,
IN CHESLEY

We beg to inform the people of Chesley and surrounding country that we have
now got our factory in running order and are prepared to ma

ALL KINDS OF FURNI URE.

We manufacture our own furniture we will be able to offer first-cla

Special Attention given
to the

**UNDERTAKING
DEPARTMENT.**

A First-Class

Hearse

Call at our ware
near Iron Railway Bridge

No. 542 Dresser

Oak. Golden. Gloss finish.
British bevel mirror, 24 x 36.
Double shaped top, 22 x 44.
Top drawers swell.
Weight, 125 lbs.

$28.00

No. 85 Centre Table

Natural Heritage/Natural History Inc.

A Century of Excellence: Krug Bros. Co. Limited
Howard Krug

Published by Natural Heritage/Natural History Inc.
P.O. Box 95, Station O, Toronto, Ontario M4A 2M8

National Library of Canada Cataloguing in Publication Data

Krug, Howard, 1904–1997.
     A century of excellence: Krug Bros. & Co. furniture manufacturers

Includes index.
ISBN 1-896219-77-2

1. Krug Bros. & Co. — History. 2. Furniture industry and trade — Ontario — Chesley — History. I. Cathcart, Ruth, 1932- II. Title.

HD9773.C34K78 2001   C2001-902836-9
338.4'76841'00971321

Natural Heritage / Natural History Inc. acknowledges the financial support of the Canada Council for the Arts and the Ontario Arts Council for our publishing program. We also acknowledge the financial support of the Government of Canada through the Book Publishing Industry Development Program (BPIDP) and the Association for the Export of Canadian Books.

Cover and text design by Derek Chung Tiam Fook
In-house editor: Jane Gibson
Printed and bound in Canada by Hignell Printing Limited, Winnipeg, Manitoba.

All visuals are from the Bruce Krug Collection unless otherwise identified.

Back Cover photo of forest by Telfer Wegg.

Dedication

To Howard Krug,
conservationist, furniture maker and mentor/brother

and to the hundreds of employees of the Krug Bros. Furniture Company,
many of whom worked well past the age of retirement
because of enjoyment and pride in their craft, and loyalty to the company.

Bruce Krug

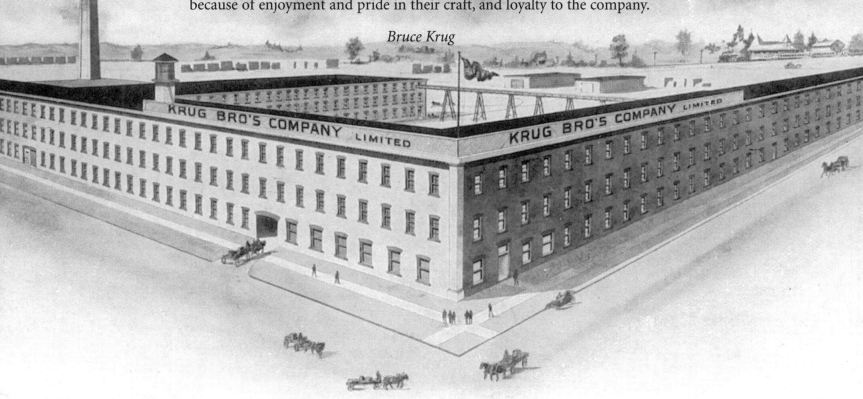

THE KRUG BROS. CO. LIMITED, CHESLEY, ONTARIO

ESTABLISHED IN 1886

Table of Contents

Preface

Howard Krug in 1978.
London Free Press, from Bruce Krug Collection.

In the summers before his final illness, while at the Krug brothers' holiday home in Tobermory, Howard Krug set down the story of the family and the enduring furniture manufacturing business which it founded. Bruce, Howard's younger brother, asked me to edit Howard's account and to plan on its publication as a memorial tribute, not only to Howard, but to the hundreds of loyal and faithful employees of Krug Bros. Co. over the years.

The story is one of a German immigrant family in Canada who demonstrated grit, intelligence, initiative, flexibility and a strong work ethic. Two generations of Krug men and women created and then carried on a large manufacturing venture over a period of 101 years from 1886 to 1987 — surviving the extreme downturn in business during WWI and the Great Depression, then meeting the overwhelming competition in the furniture trade from the United States in the post-WWII years.

The business began on a high note of optimism in 1886. Canada was prospering and the Krugs were well-positioned to provide home and business furniture for a rapidly expanding population right across the continent. The factory could hardly expand fast enough. Then came the years of consolidation, and

Bruce, W.P. and Howard Krug, 1978.

perseverance through the usual vicissitudes of business.

The company was the lifeblood of the southwestern Ontario town of Chesley. The history of town and factory was intertwined. A news item in the *Chesley Enterprise*, November 1930 reads: "W. P. Krug was elected Mayor of Chesley last Friday for the 8th consecutive time by acclamation." Another item dated June 11, 1890 reads, "Sky rockets were seen five miles out of town on May 24 when Krug Bros. gave a fine display of fireworks." Or, "Conrad Krug's Sunday School class of girls known as the 'Why Not Class' gave a tea at the armouries at which they cleared $55.72" appeared on October 29, 1916. When the factory closed in 1987, townspeople set up a committee to try to find a way to convert the factory into a furniture museum — to keep alive the story of entrepreneurship and stamina in a vital industry. Regrettably, a museum consultant shot down the idea, his position based on a feasibility study which concluded that sufficient funds would not be forthcoming.

Howard Krug joined the company after his graduation from the University of Toronto in 1925. It became the central motivational force of

his life. He was there 62 years later, when to his great sadness, the enterprise ended in 1987. Howard was a man of many parts. He organized and led two boys' clubs, which did service work throughout the community. He was actively involved on the executive of the Ontario Furniture Manufacturers' Association for many years, was a life member of the Bruce Historical Society and an honorary member of the Bruce Genealogical Society and the Saugeen Field Naturalists. As well, he was a charter member of the Bruce Trail Organization and supervised a crew from the Chesley area who spent their weekends in helping to seek out and mark the portion of the Trail from Dyer's Bay to Tobermory. In his personal life, physical activity was important; he was an ardent skier, tennis player and curler.

The study of nature was an important part of Howard's life. When he was very young, he built and erected nesting boxes for birds. In the 1930s, when the bluebird was almost extinct in the Chesley area, he established a chain of nesting boxes and succeeded in bringing much-loved bluebirds back to the area. Between 1960 and 1980, he erected bluebird boxes in the northern part of the Bruce Peninsula, re-establishing their population there. In addition, he banded several species of birds, including herring and ring-billed gulls on the islands off

the shores of the Bruce Peninsula and Manitoulin Island.

Howard Krug's deepest and most abiding interest lay in the proper use and conservation of woodlots. He understood and supported the concept of sustained yield at a time when most others were exploiting natural resources. According to E.F. "Pud" Johnston, District Forester, Bruce Peninsula and Owen Sound, "When he logged bushes, whether purchased or company owned, he always did it in a way that would assure another cut in 15 or 20 years. Howard was a pioneer and a leader in reforestation in Bruce and Grey counties." Howard and Bruce Krug have donated the Kinghurst Tract of 600 acres of old growth forest to The Federation of Ontario Naturalists. The land will be left in perpetuity as a nature reserve for the people of Ontario.

In the 1980s, when so many furniture factories in the area were closing because of lack of business, Howard Krug came to the rescue of Krug Bros. by selling personal securities to help finance operations of the business when the banks refused further assistance.

Bruce Krug, fifteen years younger than Howard, was his brother's partner throughout Howard's life. They pursued many of the same life goals and both became accomplished naturalists. Bruce, in particular, was proficient at hunting and trapping. The brothers built winter bonfires for outdoor meals, summer bonfires for corn roasts and camped in all seasons. They swam in the local swimming hole, helped on the family dairy farm and worked in the summers at the sawmill.

Throughout his life, Bruce has had an indefatigable interest in the recording and collecting of local and national history. His wide ranging interests in collecting include photography, books, postcards and a huge array of artifacts relating to the daily lives of our pioneers.

Howard and Bruce Krug have added immeasurably to the richness of life in Ontario and in Canada.

This work is developed from the original manuscript written by Howard Krug.

Ruth Cathcart, Editor

Bruce Krug in 1997.

Howard and Bruce Krug, 1978.

CHAPTER 1

Family History

Peter Krug was born in 1836, son of Peter Krug at Schwarz, state of Hesse, Alsfelt, Germany. He came to Canada in 1852. His father was a well-to-do hotel keeper in Schwarz but Peter had two reasons for leaving home. He wanted to get away from German military service and he wanted to escape a marriage that his parents were trying to arrange between himself and a rich farmer's daughter who was not to his liking.

As other Krugs of his native community had gone to Tavistock, Ontario, a growing community set in Oxford County, about 15 miles southeast of Stratford, Peter made this his first stopping place in Canada. From here he went to Berlin, Ontario, where he took employment with the Hibner Furniture Co. and learned the trade of cabinetmaker.

While Peter was working in Berlin, he met Anna Lypert of southeast Hope township near Tavistock and they were married around 1858 in Waterloo. As his wife wanted to be nearer to her relatives in the Tavistock area, they soon settled at Balaclava, a hamlet about a mile north of Tavistock. Here Peter started a small cabinetmaker's shop in a log shed attached to their house. He did every type of woodwork, including making coffins which were in demand

Home of Anna Lypert and Peter Krug at Balaclava, near Tavistock, Ontario, circa 1860. The log shed was his first shop.

from such a shop in those days. All the work was done with hand tools, including wood turning with a manually powered turning lathe. Peter's sons, as soon as they became old enough, provided the power while he did the turning.

While living in Balaclava, six children were born to the couple — Annie, John, Christian and Conrad (twins) born in 1863, William and George. For a few years Peter left the cabinetmaking trade and, sometime around the mid-1870s, he moved his family about 80 miles north to Walkerton, Ontario, to engage in the manufacture of "tow" for the upholstery trade, in an attempt to bolster his income. Tow, made from the stalk of the flax plant, was a filling for upholstered furniture, replacing horse hair which was prickly and uncomfortable. The flax stalks had to be pulled from the earth by hand as

Anna and Peter Krug and family while they were still living in Listowel, Ontario, 1885. Standing (l to r): Conrad, John, Christian, William. Seated (l to r): Annie, Peter, George and Anna (Lypert).

the better fibre was near the roots, thus making a very labour intensive process. In the 1880-81 *Directory of Bruce County*, Peter Krug is listed as a manufacturer in Walkerton. This business, however, did not prove successful, failing in about 1878. As the enterprise was not incorporated, everything, except some personal property, was seized for the creditors. Peter had to start again from the beginning.

Fortunately for the Krug family, Peter and a Mr. Hess had learned the cabinetmaking trade together in the Hibner plant in Berlin (renamed Kitchener during World War I). While Peter had been pursuing other opportunities, Hess, in the meantime, had started a successful furniture factory and was now employing around 60 men in Listowel, Ontario. At this time, the town, located on the Maitland River, served a prosperous farming community. Aware of his colleague's success, Peter wrote to him and was offered a job. The Krug family moved to Listowel in 1878 with whatever belongings the bailiff had allowed them to keep. Included in these possessions was the family cow. Christian and Conrad, the 15 year-old twin sons, walked the cow from Walkerton to Listowel a distance of almost 40 miles. (The date recorded in the *Directory* and the date of the family's removal to Listowel appear contradictory but it is quite possible that this is because the information for the *Directory* took a couple of years to gather and compile before publication.)

Peter and the eldest of his sons, John, began work at the Hess factory while Christian and Conrad took on jobs at the flax mill and brewery. Eventually, the twins also obtained employment at the Hess factory and learned the cabinetmaking trade.

After completing his training, John left

Hess Furniture Factory in Listowel, circa 1884.

Main Street in Chesley circa 1886, looking north. The Town Hall with its tower is on the left. The second building on the right is the Windsor Hotel, still standing at time of publication. Much of Main Street was destroyed by fire in 1888.

Listowel for greener fields far away — a job in a furniture factory in Cleveland, Ohio. (While it is not certain, it is thought that this factory may have been the Biber Company as John resided at 83 Woodland Avenue and the Biber establishment was also located on Woodland Avenue.) Things must have been booming in the furniture industry in that city as he kept coaxing his brother Christian to also go there to work.

Christian resisted, although his younger brother William, who was learning the upholstery trade at Hess's, did go over the border for a while. There he worked for an upholstering company but soon returned to work again at the Hess factory in Listowel.

Both Christian and Conrad, ambitious young men in their early twenties, were not satisfied with the unsteady work they had at

Listowel. The furniture manufacturing trade of the time was in its infancy. Unable to sustain steady employment, the idea of starting a business of their own held much appeal and they actively began making plans. Brother John, in Ohio, even said that he would return to Canada and join them if something satisfactory were to be found.

The two brothers went to nearby Stratford and Milverton to look at prospective sites. While at Milverton, they met a relative, Kaspar Grosch, who persuaded them to visit Chesley, a rapidly growing town further north in Bruce County. Chesley had been incorporated in 1879, six years before the arrival of Conrad and Christian Krug. The town had been founded in 1858 by Adam Scott Elliot and his sons, William and John Halliday Elliot. It was they who developed water power on the Saugeen River and built the original sawmill and gristmill. By 1875, the village boasted several general stores, blacksmith shops, a shingle mill, a sash and door factory, a lime kiln, tannery, cooper shops, woollen mill, potter and a flourishing brickyard. The Grand Trunk Railway reached Chesley in 1881. By the time the Krugs arrived in 1885, the population had reached 1400.

Grosch was a partner in the firm of Grosch and Rolston; a small manufacturer of felt boots

An advertisement placed in the *Chesley Enterprise* of 1887.

on the south side of the river running through the heart of Chesley. His factory was operated by water power provided by a dam built at the site. However, at the time, the felt boot business was quite depressed and both of the Mssrs. Grosch and Rolston were anxious to dispose of their water power site. The Krug brothers might indeed find the location to their liking.

It would be February of 1886 before Christian and Conrad boarded the train to come

The home of Peter and Anna Krug at 72 High Street, Chesley, circa 1890. Shown to the left is Anna Krug. Of the remaining women, one is Mrs. John Krug (Annie Heiserman), and one is Mrs. Annie Ankenmann. Standing by the porch is Christian Krug, with Peter Krug to the left. The house is still occupied today.

to Chesley to look over the site. Favourably impressed, they could see the potential for a future enterprise. On each side of the river stood a waterwheel. Immediately, they made arrangements to purchase one-half of the water power, one waterwheel and a building site on the north side of the river. Convinced that this would be a successful venture, they walked upstream along side of the Saugeen River to nearby Scone to order the material for their first factory from the Bearman Sawmill. On their return journey to Listowel, they discussed the advisability of carrying on with this new venture. But, despite any misgivings, they concluded that it was not possible to back out now. After all, they had given their word at the Bearman Mill that they would take the timbers and lumber that they had ordered.

The twins acted on their commitment. They contacted John asking him to return from Ohio and collected their back wages from the Hess Furniture Co. In those days, it seems that the custom in many businesses was to pay only part of the wages in cash, with the rest being retained by the employer to help finance the business. Since their brother-in-law, Henry Ankenmann, who had married Annie Krug, was also working at Hess's, they persuaded him to join in this new venture.

On May 18, 1886, Mr. and Mrs. John Krug, (by now John had married Annie Heiserman of the United States) and Mr. and Mrs. Henry Ankenmann and the bachelor brothers, Christian and Conrad Krug, all arrived in Chesley to start the business. Their furniture-making company would help to furnish many homes across Canada in the years to come. A couple of months later, their parents and two younger brothers, William and George, joined

them in the village.

Eventually, all built substantial houses in Chesley on High and River streets. Each home was linked to the factory for water, telephone and electricity.

Several of the brothers and several of their sons were active in the life of the community.

The residence of Conrad and Annie (Wenzel) Krug, built on High Street in Chesley, circa 1893. Shown are Annie, S.S. Nash (a friend), Conrad and a young Wellington, standing on the picket fence. Sitting on the balcony is Barbara Wenzel.

Conrad and Annie Krug in front of their home on High Street, with son Wellington at the wheel, 1907. A new cement sidewalk is now in place and the picket fence has been removed.

Conrad became the first mayor. His brother Christian supported baseball and hockey. John and William were active in the church and Sunday school.

Several members of the next generation entered the family business after graduation from university and gaining other life experience. John Krug's son, William Peter, graduated from the University of Toronto and then enlisted in the Canadian Expeditionary Force to Siberia. After his return he worked for a wholesale hardware firm in Windsor — eventually returning to Chesley to act as the company bookkeeper. He would become mayor of the community for many years. His brother, Stanley, attended the University of Toronto, graduating in chemical engineering, and then went overseas to serve in World War I. After the war he went to work for a chemical company in Montreal before returning to the fold to take charge of the shipping department of the family business.

Christian Krug's oldest son, Wilfred, graduated in Commerce from the University of Toronto and returned to the company to set up a cost system. He eventually left the furniture business to establish an investment office, first in Detroit and finally in Windsor.

Wilfred's younger brother, Howard, the writer of this account, led his 1926 graduating class in Forestry at the University of Toronto. Howard moved through every department of the business that became the central focus of his life. His brother Bruce relates that Howard began

Chesley's First Town Council with Conrad Krug, the first Mayor and W.A. Crow, the Reeve, 1907-1908. Top row (l to r): R.J. Follis, C.J. Mickle, Wm. McDonald; centre left: J.O. Stinson; centre right: Wm. Fishleigh; bottom row: Geo. Harrison, Alex Brenner, Jas. Grant and Wm. Halliday.

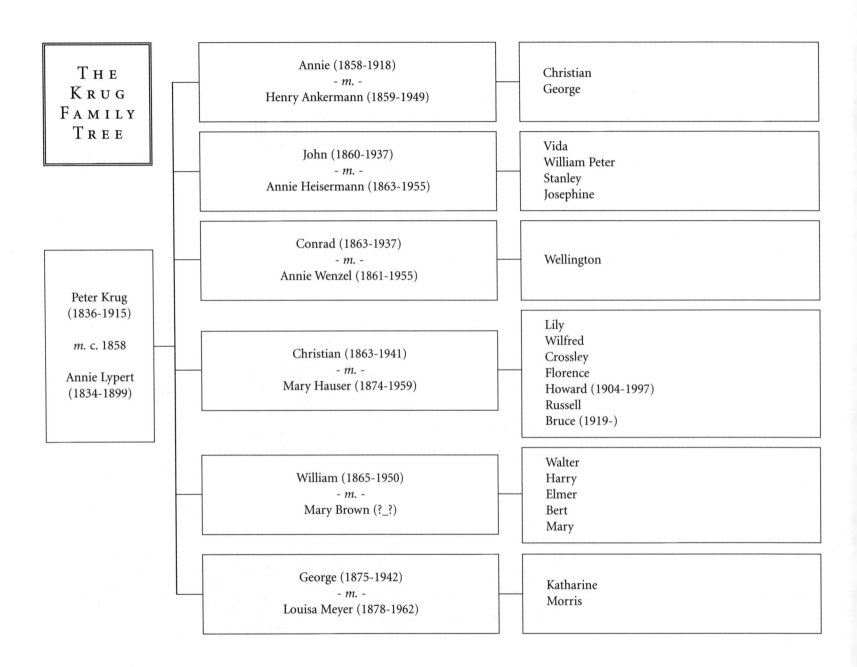

THE KRUG FAMILY TREE

Peter Krug
(1836-1915)

m. c. 1858

Annie Lypert
(1834-1899)

Annie (1858-1918)
- m. -
Henry Ankermann (1859-1949)

Christian
George

John (1860-1937)
- m. -
Annie Heisermann (1863-1955)

Vida
William Peter
Stanley
Josephine

Conrad (1863-1937)
- m. -
Annie Wenzel (1861-1955)

Wellington

Christian (1863-1941)
- m. -
Mary Hauser (1874-1959)

Lily
Wilfred
Crossley
Florence
Howard (1904-1997)
Russell
Bruce (1919-)

William (1865-1950)
- m. -
Mary Brown (?_?)

Walter
Harry
Elmer
Bert
Mary

George (1875-1942)
- m. -
Louisa Meyer (1878-1962)

Katharine
Morris

This house on Fourth Street, shown here circa 1950, was originally built for Christian and Anna (Hauser) Krug. It served as the family home for both Howard and Bruce Krug.

Bruce and Howard Krug, 1978. *Owen Sound* Sun Times, *from Bruce Krug Collection.*

in the shipping department nailing crates together. He especially enjoyed working in design, and when he became the superintendent, he could usually be found at his drafting desk. After his Uncle John died in 1937, Howard took over forest management — the purchasing of timber and logs and maintenance of the company woodlots. On the death of his father, Christian, in 1941, Howard became the company's chief executive officer retaining that position until the factory closure in 1987.

Howard's younger brother, Bruce, graduated in Biology from the University of Western Ontario in 1944. He spent three years doing fieldwork in British Columbia for the International Pacific Salmon Fisheries Commission — a joint body set up by Canada and the United States. In December 1946, Bruce returned to Chesley, in response to a request from his Uncle William, to continue family leadership of the business.

In the 1920s, Conrad's son, Wellington, and Henry Ankenmann's son, Christian, were set up in business by Krug Bros. in the Chesley Chair Co. now Crate Designs, which is still in operation in Chesley. Lil Krug, daughter of Christian, married Al Siegrist who worked as a salesman for Krug Bros. George Ankenmann, son of Henry, was in charge of the rubbing department, last stage in the finishing department of the business. For the hand rubbed finish, they used sandpaper, pumice and oil.

It is clear that the Krug Bros. was conceived and operated as a "family" business — one that was held closely by two generations of male family members. They cherished this enterprise and maintained the required family harmony to ensure its ongoing success.

CHAPTER 2

Early Buildings and Equipment

Erection of the first Krug factory building began in the early summer of 1886 on the north side of the Saugeen River, across the bridge and dam from where the Rolston's sawmill stood for many years. This new industry starting in the village interested the people of Chesley, and quite a number of the men came to assist in putting up the three-storey frame building. When completed, it measured 52 feet by 36 feet. Power was produced by the waterwheel the twins had purchased on that side of the river. Work proceeded rapidly and, on August 25, 1886, the manufacturing of furniture commenced. As there was no electricity available

at that time, coal oil lanterns provided lighting whenever daylight coming through the windows was insufficient.

Since the manufacture of early Canadian pine furniture had already yielded to furniture made of hardwood, with the advent of furniture-making machinery, the company began producing furniture from cherry, birch, maple, oak and walnut. The cherry, maple and birch were purchased from neighbouring mills, but the walnut and oak had to come from the United States, mainly from upper New York State. The need for dry lumber for furniture made it necessary to immediately construct a

The Krug Bros. factory showing the completed second building to the right of the photograph. In the background is the Grand Trunk Railway bridge spanning the North Saugeen River. It was built in 1882. The sawn lumber would have come from the nearby local sawmill.

alarm, which soon assembled a large crowd. There were some hearty workers among them who fought desperately to subdue the flames which they managed to do after the roof had been burned off and a quantity of lumber destroyed. There were 8,000 ft. of cherry and birch in the kiln, a large quantity of which was saved. Mssrs. Krug's loss is $100."

In spite of this early fire, the business carried on. By March of that year, the company had begun the manufacture of chairs and was considering the addition of a second building. Only four months later, in July, preparations were underway to erect another substantial three-storey building, this time 30 feet by 60 feet, on the same side of the river but slightly upstream from the first structure. On August 3, the frame was raised. A bell tower was added to the southeast corner of the building in August 1888. A bell, formerly used in a church in the Markdale area and still in the Krug family possession, was suspended in this tower to be rung to call the employees to work. Six years later, in the winter of 1893, a steam whistle would succeed it.

The two buildings were brought together by a bridge completed in January 1889, joining the top floor of the main building and the finishing room on the top floor of this second

heating plant and dry kiln, both of which were built north and west of the main factory building. Unexpectedly, misfortune struck the new enterprise less than a year after its opening. In January 1887, fire partially destroyed the kiln. The *Chesley Enterprise* of January 12, 1887 reported:

"About 9 o'clock last Saturday night, the dry kiln at Krug Bros. Furniture factory was observed to be on fire. Mssrs. Steven Bros. had steam up at their planing mill and thus was able to blow an

building. The demand for furniture was such that a second Barber waterwheel, made in Meaford, Ontario, was installed on the north side of the river in January 1890.

In August 1891, Krug Bros. purchased the Rolston property on the south side of the river, ensuring complete control of the available waterpower. The operations of the felt mill, which was located on site, were discontinued. The Krug company now had a sawmill to produce its own lumber on that side of the river.

With the business continuing to flourish, Krug Bros. planned to extend the finishing and shipping building on the north side of the river during 1891. James Robinson was given the contract the following year to erect this fairly large addition. That same year, 1892, the first elevator was installed for the machine and cabinet section of the factory. Further expansion took place two years later in the fall of 1894,

when an additional frame extension of 30 feet by 50 feet was added to the east end of the finishing and shipping department. Already more warehouse space was needed. As the business continued to flourish, in September 1896 a new 48-inch Barber waterwheel was installed on the north side of the river to replace the original wheel.

A new warehouse which included an upholstering room was erected on the south side of the river in August 1898. This was a two-storey frame building running from Mill Street north — a portion of which stood until the summer of 2001. A 60-foot addition was attached to this building in the spring of 1901. This addition extended west, along Mill Street, from the other building.

The office, which had been in a separate building on the south side of the river, was now moved into the west end of this new building. The ceiling of this office was finished with a fancy pressed metal, a tin ceiling which was the style of stores and offices around the turn of the century. A modern vault for the safekeeping of records

When Krug Bros. began manufacturing at the North Saugeen River site in 1886, they had only the north side of the river and half of the power sites on the dam. At this auction sale, they purchased the property on the south side of the river and the balance of the power sites.

A winter view of employees at Krug Bros. in 1891. The bridge joining the two buildings is visible in the background.

was installed with the office. On the main floor, the section east of the office became the mattress department. Beaver hay, a type of coarse grass used in the production of low-priced mattresses, was stored on the second floor.

The original building, which had been hastily erected at the beginning of operations in 1886, was found to be settling by 1900. As it would have required considerable repair, a decision was made to erect a totally new structure on the same site. In August of that year, the machinery was moved out and the old building torn down. In only ten days, a good strong structure had been erected, the machinery back in place and work going on as usual. Now four storeys in height, this new building had a base of 60 feet by 40 feet and was of frame construction, covered with sheets of metal pressed to give the appearance of brick. A local carpenter, W.D. Clarke, was in charge. He must have been a real hustler to get the work done in such a short time.

As all freight had to be transported by horse delivery to the train station for shipment to various areas in Canada, several teams of horses were required. The stables were situated at the north end of the property on the south side of the river. Two of the early teamsters were Ernest Barkholz and Sam Curtis.

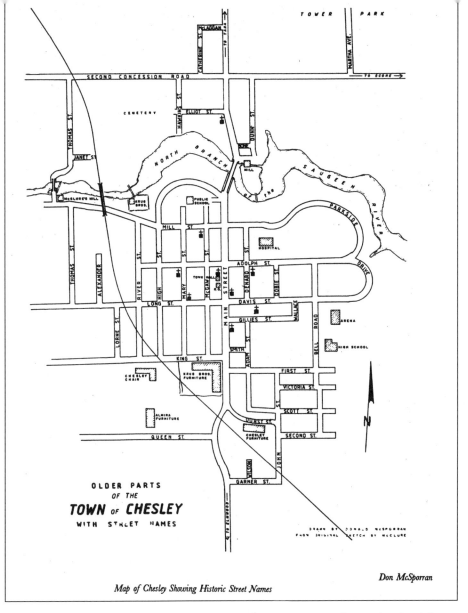

Map of Chesley Showing Historic Street Names

A map of Chesley, circa 1920, showing the Krug Bros. location on the south side of the river and the "new" factory on Main Street. The map was drawn by Don McSporran from an original sketch by McLure.

In their first decade and a half of business, from 1886 to 1900, Krug Bros. had experienced a dizzying rate of growth — a rate which was to continue until the advent of WWI. Furniture manufacture proved to be an essential industry in a rapidly expanding colony.

A group shot of the Krug Bros. employees, circa 1900. On the lower right (l to r): Peter Krug (father, with white beard), Conrad Krug, unidentified boy, Peter Moss. Below: George Krug and Christian Krug. Names of men known to be in this photograph include: Charles Monk, Louis Wenzel, Geo. Miller, Wm. Damm, Chas. Green, Gotleib Plummer, Winer Plummer, Rus. Maxwell, Sam Brugeman, Jas. Steeds, Fred Christopher, Harry Moss, ___ Hamel, John Elder, ___ Portus, ___ Wolfe, Jake Weick, Daddy Weick, Peter Krug, Henry Krug, Henry Ankenmann, John Hauser, George Haylock. The photograph was taken by J.T. Craig of Chesley.

The replacement Krug factory buildings on the north shore of the Saugeen River, 1894. Their sawmill is in the foreground. People can be seen standing at the entrance to the bridge joining the two buildings. The Pommer house, seen on the hill, has since been demolished. The railway bridge is to the upper left.

Henry Haug of Chesley, a teamster for Krug Bros., shown with his fine team of Percherons, circa 1935. The photograph was taken in front of the factory on King and Main streets.

CHAPTER 3

The Provision of Power

As has been mentioned, a water power site and dam was what attracted the original members of the Krug company to Chesley. This was the first power used to operate the line shaft from which belts were run to activate the machinery. However, it was not long until a steam engine was installed to supplement the water power.

When the manufacturing facilities were moved from the river plant to Main Street in 1911, a direct current transmission line was run from the dynamo at the dam to the new factory so that both types of power, steam and electricity, were used to run the line shafts in the plant. As the operations grew, the steam engine was replaced with a larger one at various times. Unfortunately, a full record of these changes has not been kept. However, one of the changes, shortly after moving to the Main Street site, was the purchase of a 200-horsepower Goldie McCulloch Wheelock engine #906 that was used until 1959. As the cylinder had developed some small cracks, an engine of the same size but a somewhat later model, a #989, was found to be for sale at the Beatty Bros. river plant at Fergus, Ontario. This engine was purchased and installed as a replacement. Since the 14-foot flywheels were similar, the flywheel from engine

Christian, Conrad and John Krug with their first generator, 1894, installed in the factory on the north side of the river. A big day — the first electrical power for the plant.

#906 was retained.

About 1975, it was realized that a new set of intake and exhaust valves was required for the engine and, as they were no longer available from the manufacturers, the only alternative was to make them. Some casting patterns and blueprints were obtained from Babcock-Willcox at Galt, [now part of Cambridge], and Louis Vanslyke made new patterns for the engine. The Orangeville foundry then made the castings for the valves. The machining turned out to be quite a complicated job. As much as possible was done in the home plant and what could not be done here was jobbed out mostly to Barfoot Machine Shop at Wiarton.

In the early days, water power was very important. It is interesting to note that even the small water power generating plant on Elliot's millrace was utilized and the direct current power was used to run part of the factory. This millrace had been hand-dug by John H. Elliot in the very early days of industrial development in Chesley.

As there was no large utilities company like the HEPC (Hydro Electric Power Commission, the public utilities corporation initiated by Sir Adam Beck), to provide electricity at the time, power had to be generated locally either by steam engine or by water power. Such a shortage of power must have worried the Krugs. By 1910, they were looking for an additional source of energy on the north branch of the Saugeen River. A place, about a mile west of Chesley where there were hills on both banks of the river, looked like a natural place for a dam. Subsequent investigations showed that a fall of about 40 feet could be obtained if a dam were built there. Consequently, all of the property that would be flooded by such a dam was purchased by Krug Bros. These properties consisted of Lots 27 & 28 on Concession II and Lot 27 on Concession I in Elderslie township. The dam was to be constructed at the line between Lots 26 and 27. A section of this land had a good stand of timber on it, especially that part on Lot 27, Concession I. In preparation for the future flooding, these trees were cut over the years 1911 to 1912, and some preliminary trenching was done at the dam site. However, a business recession struck and the project was temporarily shelved. The First World War of 1914-1918 further postponed the project.

Early in the 20th century, when the HEPC was developing its power project at Eugenia Falls in Grey County, the Beaver River was dammed in order to provide energy for the Grey/Bruce area. When heavy rains fell in June 1915, washing out the dam at nearby Scone, the source of electric power for Chesley, the town was one of the first communities in this area to sign a contract with HEPC to supply its power. According to this contract, any new power lines on the town streets were restricted to those belonging to this power commission. Such a restriction prohibited access of the power from the North Saugeen dam project and no further work was done on it. The land, however,

remained in Krug hands.

When the business was operating at the river site, there were two 48-inch waterwheels on the north side of the river and one 60-inch waterwheel on the south side. These wheels were of the horizontal turbine type made by the Barber foundry at Meaford, Ontario. In July 1894, a new dynamo and attachments were

When Louis Vanslyke, one of Krug's engineers, was shown this photograph in 1964, he believed the steam engine to be a Wheelock, likely the one which had been removed from Krug Bros. Co. Ltd. in July 1959. William Peter (W.P.) Krug, John Krug's oldest son, suggested that this was the engine purchased by Krug Bros. about 1912, from a plant at the south end of Mount Forest, Ontario. He remembered going there with several members of the firm to look at an engine. As he recalled, the building had been dismantled and the engine was sitting there by itself.

Howard and Bruce Krug just prior to dismantling the Wheelock Engine #906 at Krug Bros. in Chesley, during July 1959.

THE KRUG BROS. CO. LIMITED, CHESLEY, ONTARIO

ESTABLISHED IN 1886

This rendition of the new Main Street factory, originally built in 1911, was frequently used in the Krug Bros. catalogues. The last remnants of the once-handsome structure was demolished in the summer of 2001, truly the end of an era.

purchased for $375 and these were installed to generate electricity for lighting the buildings. This was much more efficient and less hazardous than the coal oil lamps that were formerly used. This innovation at the factory was soon extended to the Krug and Ankenmann homes, four of which were on River Street with the other two nearby on High Street. However, this luxury was available only when the factory was not operating. As the working day was ten hours, the lights in the homes did not come on until after 6 o'clock in the evening, or not at all if the water in the millpond was too low.

Howard Krug well remembered that with

Tom Brownscombe and Louis Vanslyke, preparing to dismantle the Wheelock Engine #906. Very important people within the Krug operation, they kept the engine in tip-top shape. Louis would make patterns for engine parts and these would be made in the foundry in Orangeville.

the shorter daylight hours of autumn and winter, coal oil lamps and candles were used in the afternoons before 6 pm and in the mornings after 7 am. Also, most of the electric lights in the homes would burn all night, as there was no automatic controller to take care of surplus power at the dynamo if the house lights were turned off.

When operations were moved to the new plant in 1911, a power line was run along River Street across to the factory to supply direct current for the operation of machinery and lights. When HEPC became available in 1916, the lighting system at the factory was soon changed over. Also, the noticeable shortage of power from the river led to one of the main line shafts being converted to HEPC power. It was fortunate that, at the time when most plants were installing 220 to 440-volt power, the Krug factory owners were advised to put in the more satisfactory 60 cycle, 550-volt system.

For some time, the factory operated with the three sources of power — the line shaft from the steam engine, the line shaft run from the HEPC power and the line shafts operated by the direct current from the river dam. As more motorized equipment was purchased, it would always be with alternating current power. Ultimately, the factory became less and less dependent on direct current from the river until this was discontinued altogether around 1920.

In 1923, the building with the power plant on the north side of the river was leased to R.J. and Herb Rannie who started manufacturing basswood excelsior there. (Excelsior is a finely shredded wood used as packing material). However, this proved to be a short-lived venture, ending in April 1924 when the four-storey building was destroyed by fire. The fire also damaged the framework over the waterwheels and put an end to developing power on the north side of the river. Now the dam was used only for supplying water to the turbine on the south side of the river to operate the sawmill. This operation continued until the sawmill also was destroyed by fire on January 23, 1938.

The aforementioned dam was built many years ago when Chesley was in its infancy. The base of the dam, which rested on the hardpan of the riverbed, consisted of three sets of cedar timbers running across the river with alternate rows of short timbers running at right angles. These were all pinned together with steel drifts (pegs). The spaces between the timbers were filled with large boulders. The upper section of the dam was also built with timbers, which were gated to allow the water to enter the flumes to the waterwheels. Six floodgates at the centre of the dam allowed surplus water to escape. This upper section was washed away in the flood of June 1915. Fortunately, the base remained and the upper section was rebuilt. Over the years concrete was thrown in on the upper side of the base of the dam to prevent water from washing through and weakening the base. Almost every year this type of maintenance was carried out, keeping the dam in good repair. However, on March 13, 1977, a huge quantity of water was released at the Co-op dam. This particular dam was originally built about a half-mile upstream by Chesley founder, Adam Scott Elliot. The resulting extreme force washed out both the upper and the lower parts of the Chesley dam. Since it had not been used in the two years since the devastating sawmill fire of 1975, it was not rebuilt.

It is interesting to note that in the summer after the dam went out, quite a number of old logs were recovered. Some of these had been sunk for many years and still showed brand marks stamped on the ends. These were mostly KB (Krug Bros.) brand but others were the JHE brand for J.H. Elliot, son of Adam Elliot, and the TB brand for either Biette & Co. or Bearman Co. Both parties had sawmills farther up the river many years ago.

Up to 1918, the smokestacks from the boilers were made of steel. These would deteriorate every few years and, consequently, required ongoing replacements. The concrete stack which still stands was built in 1918 and gave good service for the duration of the company operations. While the sawmill was being operated by waterpower, all the sawdust and the slabs were available for burning. Coal was brought in as a supplementary fuel but, over the years, wood from the sawmill along with the waste from the factory provided the energy to keep the steam plant going.

It is no longer known who the early

engineers were who had charge of the steam power plants, but the following names come to mind as having been chief engineers at various times in the past 70 years from 1920 to 1990: Robert Lochead, George Streeter, Tom Brownscombe, Frank Elliot and Louis Vanslyke. Both Streeter and Brownscombe had worked at nearby Cargill for Henry Cargill & Son, the operators of a sawmill, planing mill, shingle mill, grist mill and woollen mill, along with a foundry. The two men came to Chesley following the slowing down and ultimate closure of operations at Cargill. A pair of new HRT boilers, 18 inches by 72 inches, had been installed in Cargill around 1914. Still in good condition, these were purchased about 1924 and moved to Chesley where Streeter and Brownscombe, who had fired them at Cargill, once again took charge. These boilers were well cared for and served until 1957 when, because of their age and the possibility of metal fatigue, their replacement was recommended.

A Dominion Bridge all-welded boiler, 18 inches by 84 inches, which had been used for 1½ years at Baden in the Livingston linseed oil factory, was purchased from Toronto Elevators Ltd. and moved to Chesley. Hunter Bridge & Boiler Co. of Kincardine installed it. To improve efficiency, this boiler was set higher than its predecessors had been, and a new building, 50 feet by 30 feet, made of cement block, was erected to house it. Krug employees, Ernest Holmes and Alfred Pratt, carried out the work. A second HRT boiler, 18 inches by 72 inches, was purchased and installed by Hunter Bridge & Boiler Co. in 1971 as a standby unit. It was never put to use.

CHAPTER 4

Capitalization and Finances

When the business was started in 1886, a partnership agreement was drawn up among the five principals, the four Krug brothers, John, Conrad, Christian and William Krug, along with the brother-in-law, Henry Ankenmann. Each contributed $500 as capital and each was to have one-fifth of the profits. It was also decided that each of the partners would be paid a wage of $6 per week. The balance of any earnings was to be plowed back into the business.

During the very early years, both manufacturing and retailing were carried out. As was then the custom, a casket business was combined with the retail furniture shop, located on the east side of Main Street The retail trade flourished. A story, which cannot be substantiated but which has persisted to this day, has it that the blame for the great Main Street fire of Chesley in 1888 can be laid at the doorstep of the owner of a competing business. The retail department of the Krug Bros. furniture business was sold to Reavley & Savage in 1896, a management decision that allowed Krug Bros. to concentrate

Chesley Advertiser, 1887.

The home of Christian and Anna Krug still stands on Fourth Street West. Built in 1899, it is shown here as it looked in 1910. The home is still occupied by a member of the Krug family. This photograph was taken by W.H. Wills of Chesley.

on the manufacture of furniture.

A private bank in Chesley, known by the name of J.H. Elliot & Co. at that time, handled all Krug banking services. Later, this bank was taken over by the Bank of Hamilton, which in turn became part of the Canadian Imperial Bank of Commerce — now known as the CIBC.

In 1894, the sum of $3,000 was subscribed by 143 citizens of the Village of Chesley and District in amounts of $1 to $150. This was a loan to the company with interest at 6%. With this loan the company was obligated to carry on business on the Chesley premises for a minimum of ten years. It is thought that this undertaking by the people of Chesley was the result of attempts by other towns to lure the business to their communities. It is known that both Brampton and Listowel had been trying to attract Krug Bros. to their communities at about this time.

On May 21, 1896, a totally new partnership agreement was drawn up with the interest of the five partners divided as follows: John Krug — $10,085.06, Conrad Krug — $8,924.16, Christian Krug — $10,256.92, William Krug — $9,601.49 and Henry Ankenmann — $9,562.59. The firm continued under the name Krug Bros. & Co. until 1909 when it was incorporated as The Krug Bros. Co. Ltd., with a capital of 3,000 shares valued at $100 per share and a board of directors. The four older brothers and Henry Ankenmann each owned 300 shares. George Krug, the youngest brother who by now had joined the company, had 60 shares. The remaining shares were not issued.

On April 2, 1931, Krug Bros. received a Dominion Charter, giving the company permission to sell its furniture in all Canadian provinces. Each province required a payment from the company. As this new status required a change in the name, the company became Krug Bros. Co'y Limited. The five senior members received 400 shares each and George received 80 shares.

The name of the company would remain the same until its final days, with Krug family retaining ownership. Howard Krug, son of Christian, was the CEO for the last 46 years of the life of the company.

CHAPTER 5

Early Designs in Furniture

The earliest extant company catalogue is for 1892. The wording at the beginning of the publication, reads, "We hope you will like our new style catalogue," suggesting that there must have been at least one earlier version. It is interesting to note that an 1885 Hess Furniture Company catalogue shows similarities in design to the designs shown in the 1892 Krug catalogue. This, however, is not surprising when it is remembered that it was at the Hess Company that the brothers received their training.

Walnut was a popular wood at the time and a considerable amount of walnut lumber was used in these early designs. Often walnut burl overlays were used for decorative purposes. The style of this furniture could be termed as late Victorian of Eastlake design, a late Victorian (c. 1880-1910 in Canada) style in furniture named after Charles Locke Eastlake, the English author of *Hints on Household Taste in Furniture, Upholstery and Other Details*, published in 1868.

While bedroom and dining room furniture have always been the main types of furniture manufactured in Chesley, a much wider line was part of the earlier years. An 1892 invoice shows that a barber's chair had been made and shipped to Durham, Ontario. As well, upholstered furniture remained an important line until around 1920, and springs and mattresses were part of their product until about the beginning of WWI. Then, as part of the war effort, the company manufactured munitions boxes. Following the war, specialist upholstery factories began to appear and took over this aspect of manufacturing. As a consequence, Krug Bros. discontinued this particular line of work and concentrated their efforts on furniture.

Church furniture, including pulpits, pedestals, chairs and communion tables, was a line shown in the earliest catalogues. In fact, church furniture was made until about the sixties, when it had to be discontinued because of a diminishing demand. During the time of the boom in fraternal lodges, the manufacture of lodge furniture was also a significant part of the Krug operations. Right across Canada, many of these groups still have furniture produced in Chesley. For both the church and lodge furniture, quartered white oak was almost always used.

In the earliest years of manufacture, walnut, and other woods finished as walnut and

William Heiserman, a brother-in-law of John Krug, with a sideboard popular in 1892. He designed and built a limited number of these sideboards. The retail price at that time was $45.00.

An oak hall stand with an umbrella holder on the right and a beautiful bevelled mirror, 1896.

A student's rocker, Krug catalogue, 1894.

On facing page:
A walnut parlour suite, from Catalogue 18, Krug Bros. & Co., Furniture Manufacturers, 1904.

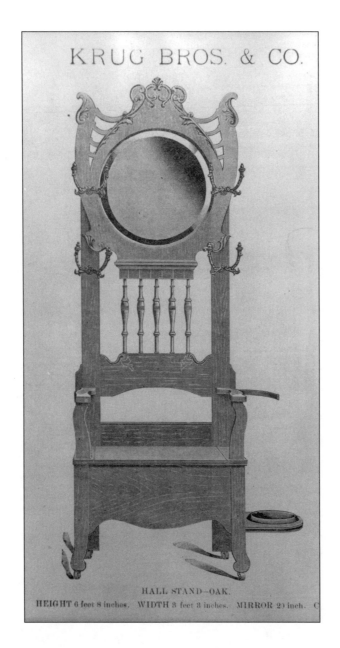

KRUG BROS. & CO.

HALL STAND—OAK.
HEIGHT 6 feet 8 inches.   WIDTH 3 feet 3 inches.   MIRROR 20 inch.   C

STUDENT'S ROCKER.

No. 1034. PARLOR SUITE—*Walnut.*

Lounge, Krug catalogue, 1895.

mahogany, were the most popular and much in demand as furniture. However, by the 1890s, quartered white oak became the desired furniture wood for the middle-to upper-class market. This shift in taste is clearly seen in the catalogues of 1895 and later. At the same time, in order to produce a lower-priced line of furniture that looked like quartered oak, "surface oak" was developed. This grained finish on maple, beech, or birch, and sometimes on elm, was used on most of the less costly furniture until around

1920, after which time it rapidly fell out of favour. Furniture with this type of finish appears nowadays in antique shops, where it is often referred to as "poor man's oak."

For designs in a price range that sat between the true quartered oak and surface oak, plain sawn red and white oak was popular. Most of these designs had multiple spindle carvings, especially on the mirror frames and bed ends, for decorative effect.

In 1902, patent #77268 was taken out by

Christian Krug for "Improvements in Furniture or Cabinet Drawers." In this proposal, the drawer was suspended and guided by a raised side guide attached to the furniture case, which ran along grooves on the outside surface of the drawer sides. This guide was used for about 25 years. It is this feature that can help to identify most of the Krug furniture of that period. Later, centre drawer controls were introduced. This was considered a better system of guiding and the company adopted it as part of their design. Some of the older pieces of furniture in the Krug Collection in the Bruce County Museum reveal the patented drawer guide, referred to as the "relished guide" and shown in the patent papers.

It is interesting to note that machine-dovetailed drawers were used from at least 1887. A table made in 1887 and a bedroom suite made in 1889 in the Krug Collection illustrate this characteristic. As these pieces have machine-dovetailed drawers, it is doubtful the Chesley factory ever had the "Clements" machine which made the pin and scallop connection. This pin and scallop dovetail was used in the interval between hand dovetailing and machine dovetailing.

For a great many years, the elm was a very common tree in the Bruce-Grey region of Ontario. It, too, became an important species for

CHAIRS.

No. 2.
HEIGHT 4 ft. 7 in.

No. 1.
HEIGHT 6 ft. 4 in.

No. 2.
HEIGHT 4 ft. 7 in.

Church furniture, Krug catalogue, 1892.

An elm bedroom suite
with a walnut finish,
shown as No. 166 in the
*Illustrated Furniture
Catalogue* printed for
Krug Bros. & Co., 1892.

J.L. JONES. TORONTO.

No. 166. SUITE—ELM.

HEIGHT OF BED 6 ft.   SLATS 50 inches.   MIRROR 18 x 36.   PLAIN.

FINISH—IMITATION WALNUT AND ANTIQUE. GLOSS FINISH.

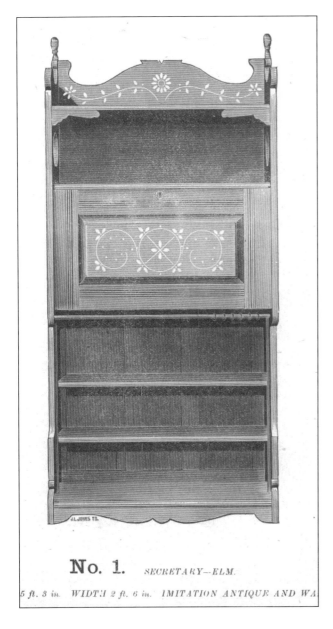

No. 1. *SECRETARY—ELM.*

5 ft. 3 in. WIDTH 2 ft. 6 in. IMITATION ANTIQUE AND WA...

KRUG BROS. & CO.

No. 36. *SIDEBOARD.—MAPLE AND ASH.*

MIRROR 22 x 28. BRITISH BEVEL.
FINISHED IN WALNUT COLOR, MAHOGANY AND ANTIQUE ASH.
HEIGHT 7 feet 2 inches. TOP 46 x 21.

An elm secretary, No. 1, 1892.

A sideboard, No. 36, made of maple and ash, but finished in walnut colour, mahogany and antique ash, 1892.

furniture manufacturing. Elm seemed more desirable than hard maple. At one time the company paid 50% more for elm than for maple ($7.50 per thousand ft. for elm as compared to $5 for maple). Christian was once asked the reason for this. His answer was that the furniture makers liked the nice, soft elm wood that came from the big trees. It was these large trees of the virgin forest that provided the soft-textured lumber that was easy to machine and glue up into panels. Later, maple took precedence — due possibly to the popularity of the "surface oak" finish on maple in the early part of the century. This finish was more adaptable to a diffuse porous wood like maple, rather than a ring porous wood like elm. Elm now dropped in price and was used only for the low-end line of furniture — especially for the low-priced single dressers and washstands much in demand at the time. Consequently, most inexpensive bedroom and dining room suites were made with elm. However, by the 1930s, elm was discontinued as a face wood because of buyer resistance. The public came to consider elm as a "cheap" wood, partly because of the so-called "fence corner" elms (the ones clearly visible in open ground). These were often distorted, twisty specimens with many knots, generally not appreciated by the consumer.

About that time, William, who was responsible for the Toronto trade, asked that the Krug dining room suites be made of gumwood, as he could get $15 more on the wholesale price of a nine-piece dining room suite if it were made in gumwood (which they imported from the Mississippi Valley) rather than elm. Then, the wholesale price of such a suite was running in the $45 to $55 price range.

During the latter part of the second decade of the 20th century, walnut finishes became popular and were applied to maple, elm, birch and gumwood furniture. As well, American black walnut lumber and veneer were imported from Pennsylvania for making both solid and veneered pieces. The solid walnut lines were extended, especially during the Depression Years, when the #1 common steamed walnut (heated in order to render the colour uniform) was being delivered for less than $100 per thousand feet. Solid walnut furniture became very popular with the trade because of an extensive advertising campaign initiated by the Gibbard Furniture Company of Napanee. However, with the end of the Depression and the higher prices brought on by the onset of World War II, walnut lumber became too expensive to acquire, except for very special pieces.

In the earliest years, a bedroom suite

A cherry and ash bedroom suite, 1892.

No. 150. *SUITE—CHERRY AND ASH.*

consisted of three pieces; a three-drawer dresser and mirror, a washstand and a bed with a headboard about seven feet high. In the 1890s, the dresser changed to a two-drawer dresser with a small cupboard and drawer on one side and a large rectangular mirror rising from the two-drawer side. This mirror usually tilted horizontally, but on the #150 suite, illustrated in the 1892 catalogue and shown in the Krug Collection, housed at the Bruce County Museum and Archives in Southampton, the swing is vertical from left to right. By the end of the 19th century, this style of dresser was giving way to the three-drawer dresser and high bed-ends were lowered to a height of about 40 inches.

In 1905, a new style of dresser began appearing in the catalogues. It was called the "Princess Dresser." It was a low two-drawer dresser with a large, oval or rectangular, framed swing mirror. This was popular until about 1912 when the style gave way to the conventional three-drawer dresser once more. Chests of drawers or chiffoniers became more important in bedroom suites. The washstand faded in popularity with the advent of indoor plumbing, and almost disappeared by the end of the 1920s. Some time between 1910 and 1920, the vanity table and the bedside table made their entrance into mainstream furniture styles. Later in the 1920s, the standard bedroom suite consisted of a three-drawer dresser, a chest of drawers, a vanity table with a stationary centre mirror and a small swinging mirror on each side, a bed and an optional bedside table.

Iron and brass beds became popular as bedroom suites from the early 1900s until around 1914. Initially, Krug Bros. & Co. imported them in carload lots from the Art Bedstead Company of Chicago for distribution to their dealers. Several pages in the 1905 catalogue illustrate various designs. In January 1906, an agreement was made with the Weston Bed Company of Weston, Ontario, whereby they agreed to sell carload lots of 15 different styles of beds to Krug Bros. & Co. This agreement was signed by Arthur Garner, who later arranged to have the industry moved to Chesley as "Canada Beds Ltd." A new building was erected on Garner Street for their manufacture.

Another notable feature of the furniture of the 1905-1915 period was the prominence of curved fronts, mostly on quartered oak pieces. Chestnut was considered to be a good wood on which to veneer because of its stability. For Krug furniture, this was the wood used for curved fronts. A block was built up from 4-inch by 4-inch lumber to the required thickness for drawer or door fronts. It was then hand-sawed to the curve and the veneer was glued to the faceside. This proved to be a satisfactory way of providing the curve. Any pieces made using this method that were later examined by experts demonstrate little warping or checking in the face of the veneer.

In dining room furniture, a suite usually consisted of a sideboard, extension table and dining chairs. In the early 1900s, the chairs were made with a decorative pattern pressed into the back rail. Today, antique dealers referred to them as "pressed-back chairs." Around 1910, this chair design was replaced with a design more in keeping with the style of the rest of the suite. About the same time, an attempt was made to bring together the design of the extension tables and sideboards.

The rectangular extension table was the type sold until the early 1900s, after which the round, pedestal extension table became popular and remained so for about 15 years. It eventually was replaced by oval and rectangular tables with corner legs.

Originally, sideboards had high backs with large mirrors and were decorated with spindles and carvings. By 1910, these mirrors were noticeably smaller and the sideboard evolved into the buffet backed by a small mirror or pediment.

As most early houses lacked closets, the wardrobe became a popular line. Both factory-assembled and knockdown styles (those which were machined but not assembled) were made regularly. Occasional tables, commodes, desks (secretaries, roll-top, and flattop), kitchen cabinets and kitchen tables were also standard items of production.

In the upholstery department, parlour sets consisting of a loveseat and side chairs were in demand in the earliest days. An early style of daybed was developed and is illustrated in the 1904 catalogue. This was a couch that unfolded to serve as a bed when required. A few years ago, one of these daybeds surfaced in the Arthur, Ontario, area. After being reupholstered by Clifford Woodcraft, it promptly sold to a discerning Toronto customer.

Today, Krug furniture is much in demand as a collectible and sells quickly at auctions.

An oak bedroom suite
No. 154 1/2, from the
*Illustrated Furniture
Catalogue* of 1896.

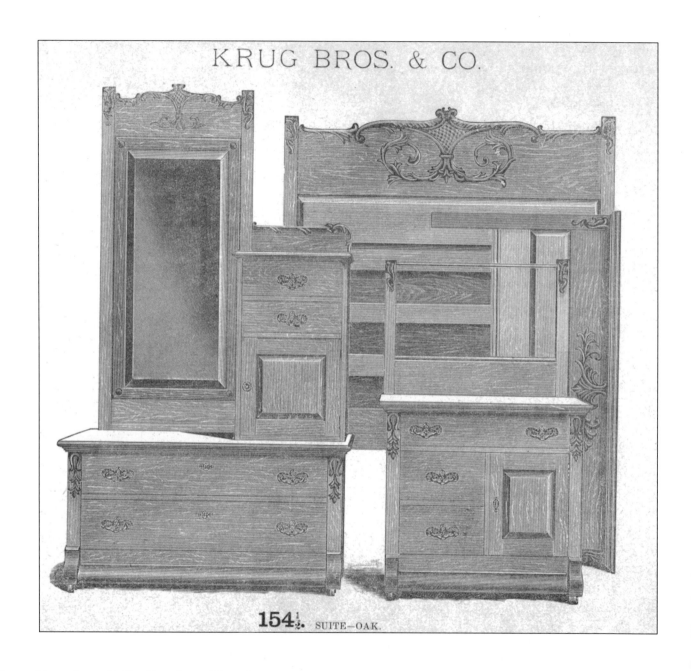

KRUG BROS. & CO.

154½. SUITE—OAK.

An oak secretary, No. 215, as displayed in the 1896 catalogue.

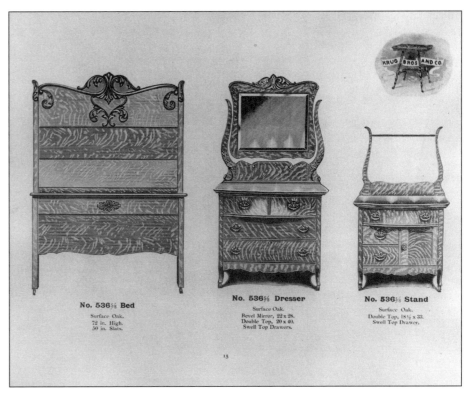

A bedroom suite finished with "surface oak" or "poor man's oak" advertised in the 1905 catalogue.

An elm cupboard, No. 3,
1896.

A desk made from elm,
No. 104, 1896.

KRUG BROS. & CO.

No. 3. CUPBOARD—ELM.

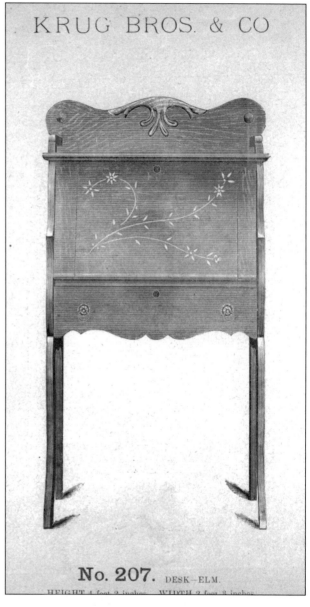

KRUG BROS. & CO

No. 207. DESK—ELM.

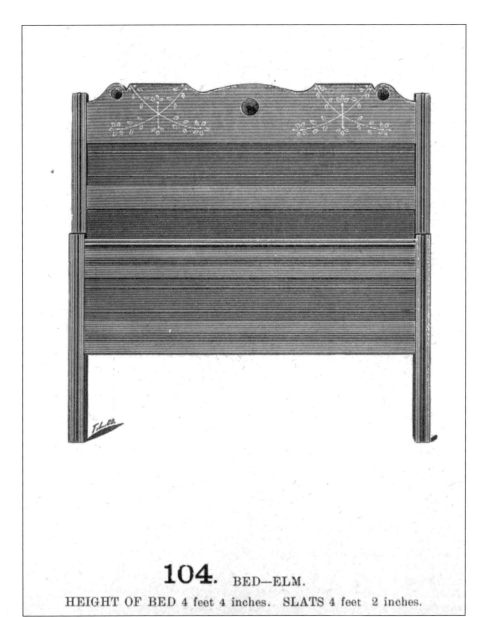

104. BED—ELM.

HEIGHT OF BED 4 feet 4 inches. SLATS 4 feet 2 inches.

Headboard No. 104
with typical desgin and
footboard as shown in
the 1896 catalogue.

An elm cupboard,
No. 309, 1896.

KRUG BROS. & CO.

No. 309. SIDEBOARD—ELM.
HEIGHT 6 feet 2 inches. TOP 46x20. MIRROR 14x24.

No. 3035—DINING ROOM SUITE
Solid Walnut.

No. 3035—BUFFET
Top, 66x21 inches. Panels in Doors and Centre
Drawer with decorated Walnut Veneer, Drawer
fitted with Sliding Tray.

No. 3035—PEDESTAL EXTENSION TABLE
Top, 42x56 inches. Extends 6 feet. Top,
Solid Walnut or 5-ply Veneer.

3035	Buffet	$ 36 00
	China Cabinet	27 00
	Extension Table, 6 ft	26 00
	Diners, per set	36 00
		————$125 00
	Extension Table, 8 ft., **$5.00** extra.	

No. 3035—CHINA CABINET
Top, 40x15 inches. Overlays not shown on
Panel.

No. 3035—ARM DINER

No. 3035—SMALL DINER

Brown or Blue Leather Slip Seats. Carvings on
top rail not showing

A solid walnut dining room suite (No. 3035) including buffet and china cabinet.

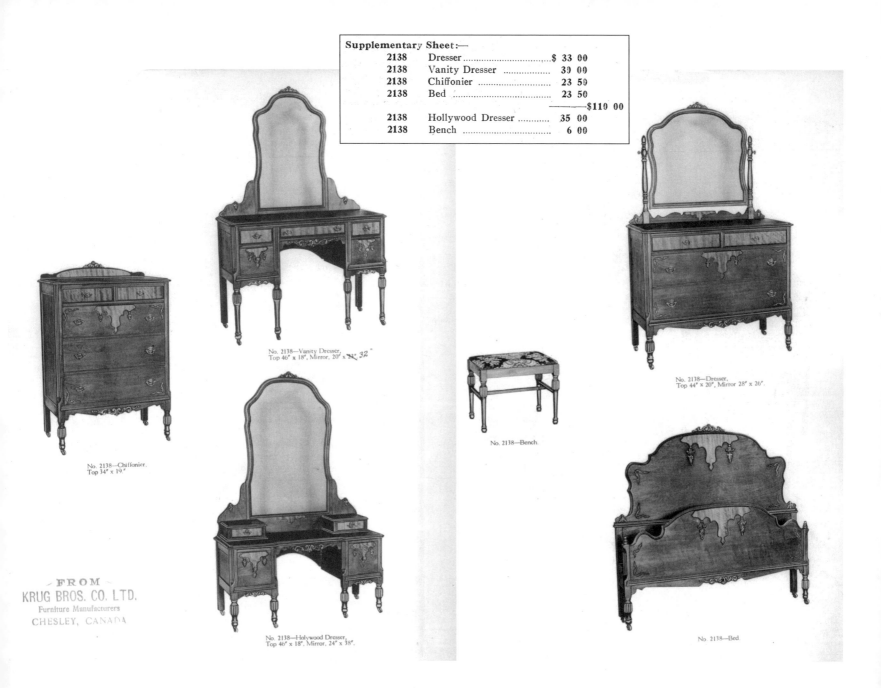

Supplementary Sheet :—		
2138	Dresser	$ 33 00
2138	Vanity Dresser	39 00
2138	Chiffonier	23 50
2138	Bed	23 50
		———$110 00
2138	Hollwood Dresser	35 00
2138	Bench	6 00

No. 2138—Vanity Dresser,
Top 46" x 18", Mirror, 20" x 32"

No. 2138—Bench.

No. 2138—Dresser,
Top 44" x 20", Mirror 28" x 26".

No. 2138—Chiffonier,
Top 34" x 19."

FROM
KRUG BROS. CO. LTD.
Furniture Manufacturers
CHESLEY, CANADA

No. 2138—Holywood Dresser,
Top 46" x 18", Mirror, 24" x 38'.

No. 2138—Bed.

On opposite page: Bedroom suite, No. 2138 made of solid black walnut with an Oriental walnut overlay.

Two style variations of oak dressers with gloss finish shown in Catalogue No. 22, published in 1907.

No. 542 Dresser

Oak. Golden. Gloss finish.
British bevel mirror, 24 x 36.
Double shaped top, 22 x 44.
Top drawers swell.
Weight, 125 lbs.

$28.00

No. 541 Dresser

Oak. Golden. Gloss finish.
British bevel mirror, 24 x 36.
Double shaped top, 22 x 44.
Top drawers swell.
Bed and stand same as No. 542.
Weight, 125 lbs.

$27.00

A bedroom suite, No. 2017, made of gumwood, includes the bedstand, a dresser and a chiffonier. According to the price list of the 1928 catalogue, this suite sold for $96.00 at the time.

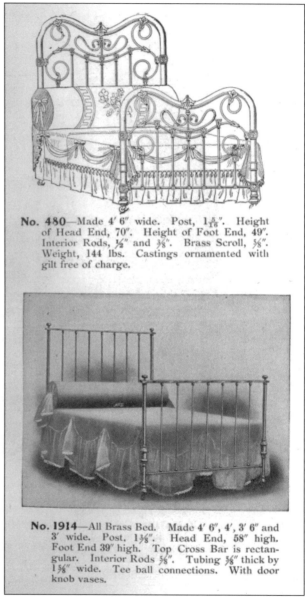

No. 480—Made 4′ 6″ wide. Post, $1\frac{5}{16}$″. Height of Head End, 70″. Height of Foot End, 49″. Interior Rods, $\frac{1}{2}$″ and $\frac{3}{8}$″. Brass Scroll, $\frac{5}{8}$″. Weight, 144 lbs. Castings ornamented with gilt free of charge.

No. 1914—All Brass Bed. Made 4′ 6″, 4′, 3′ 6″ and 3′ wide. Post, $1\frac{3}{8}$″. Head End, 58″ high. Foot End 39″ high. Top Cross Bar is rectangular. Interior Rods $\frac{5}{8}$″. Tubing $\frac{5}{8}$″ thick by $1\frac{5}{8}$″ wide. Tee ball connections. With door knob vases.

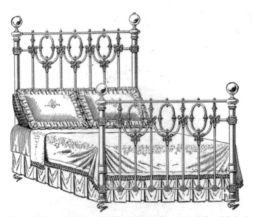

Six different styles of brass beds as shown in the 1905 catalogue.

No. 340—Made 4' 6" wide. Post, 1⁵⁄₁₆". Height of Head End, 67". Height of Foot End, 42". Interior Rods, ⅜". Brass Top Rail ¾". Ovals, ⅝". Brass Spindles, Mounts and Vases. Weight 116 lbs. Castings ornamented with gilt.

No. 900—Made 4' 6" wide. Post, 2". Height of Head End, 70". Height of Foot End 46". Interior Rods, ½" and ⁵⁄₁₆". Brass Top Rod, ¾". Brass Vases and Mounts 3½". Brass Spindles 5". Castings ornamented with gilt. Weight 165 lbs.

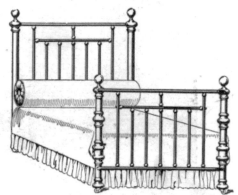

No. 1689—All Brass Bed. Made 4' 6", 4', 3' 6" and 3' wide. Post, 2", Bow Foot. Top Rods ¾". Tee Ball Trimmings. Head End, 68" high. Foot End 44" high.

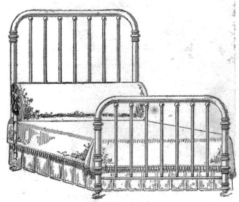

No. 1855—All Brass Bed. Made 4' 6", 4', 3' 9" and 3' wide. Post, 1⅜". Interior Rods, ⅝". Head End 63" high. Foot End, 39" high. Tee Ball Connections.

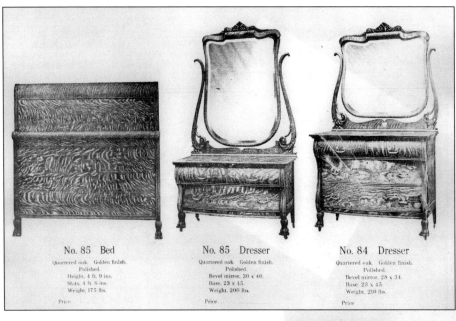

No. 85 Bed
Quartered oak. Golden finish.
Polished.
Height, 4 ft. 9 ins.
Slats, 4 ft. 6 ins.
Weight, 175 lbs.

Price ....

No. 85 Dresser
Quartered oak. Golden finish.
Polished.
Bevel mirror, 30 x 40.
Base, 23 x 45.
Weight, 200 lbs.

Price ....

No. 84 Dresser
Quartered oak. Golden finish.
Polished.
Bevel mirror, 28 x 34.
Base, 23 x 45.
Weight, 210 lbs.

Price ....

A quartered oak
bedroom suite featuring
a curved front on each
of the two styles of
dressers, 1910.

A sample of a press-
back diner chair,
armchair and arm
rocker from the 1915
catalogue.

No. 90—Diner   No. 91—Armchair   No. 93—Arm Rocker

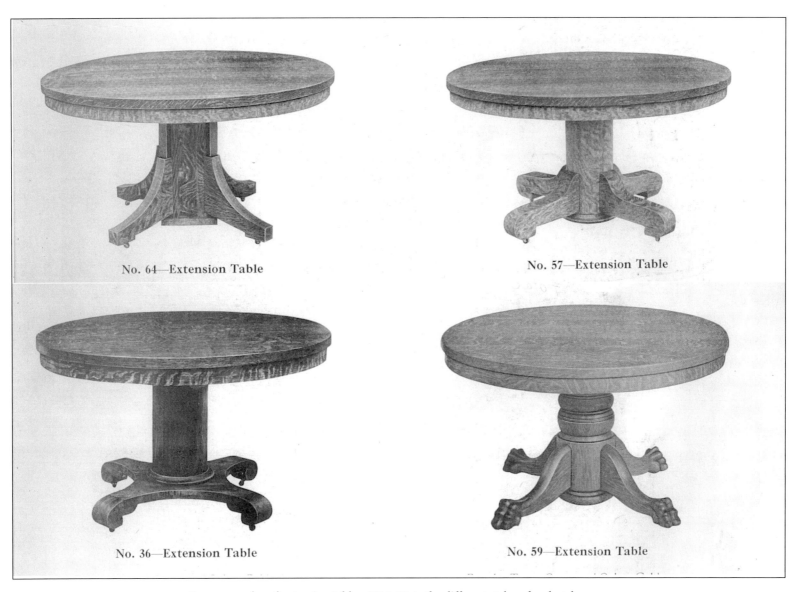

No. 64—Extension Table

No. 57—Extension Table

No. 36—Extension Table

No. 59—Extension Table

Four examples of extension tables, 1915. Note the different styles of pedestals.

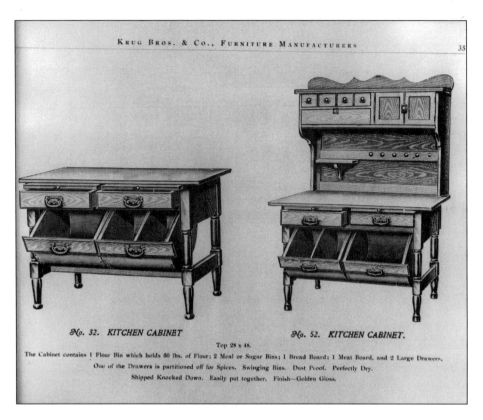

No. 32. KITCHEN CABINET

No. 52. KITCHEN CABINET.

Top 28 x 48.

The Cabinet contains 1 Flour Bin which holds 60 lbs. of Flour; 2 Meal or Sugar Bins; 1 Bread Board; 1 Meat Board, and 2 Large Drawers.

One of the Drawers is partitioned off for Spices. Swinging Bins. Dust Proof. Perfectly Dry.

Shipped Knocked Down. Easily put together. Finish—Golden Gloss.

Two different styles of kitchen cabinets, from the catalogue of 1902.

No. 267—Roll-top Desk

Oak.   Golden or Fumed.
Bed Polished.
Automatic Locks on Drawers.
Top, 30 x 42.
Height, 48 inches.
Shipped knock-down.
Weight, 180 lbs.

Three variations of roll-top desks, 1915.

No. 269—Desk

Oak. Polished. Golden or Fumed.
Top, 30 x 54.
Height, 50 inches.
Shipped knock-down.
Depth, 30 inches.
Automatic Locks on Drawers.
Weight, 300 lbs.

No. 268—Roll-top Desk

Oak. Golden or Fumed Finish.
Height, 48 inches.
Length, 50 inches.
Depth, 30 inches.
Automatic Locks on Drawers.
Shipped knock-down.
Weight, 180 lbs.

No. 85 Morris Chair

Quartered Front and Arms.
Golden. Polished.
Loose Reversible Cushions.

No. 220 Morris Chair

Quarter-Sawed Oak.
Mission Style.
Loose Reversible Cushions.

Morris chair #85 and a Mission style Morris chair #220, as displayed in the 1905 catalogue.

No. 78 Centre Table

Quartered Oak.   Top, 24 x 28.
Golden Oak.   Polished.
Shipped Knocked Down.

No. 85 Centre Table

Quartered Oak.   Top, 23 x 23.
Golden Oak.   Polished Top and Shelf.
Shipped Knocked Down.

No. 78 Table

Quartered Oak.   Top, 15 x 15.
Golden Oak Finish.   Polished Top and Shelf.
Shipped Knocked Down.

65

No. 17 Writing Desk

Ash. Golden Gloss Finish. Top 60 x 30.
Top covered with imitation leather. Shipped Knocked Down.

No. 19 Desk

Ash. Golden Gloss Finish.
Top 44 x 30.

Two writing desks, both made of ash, 1905.

Two styles of wardrobes, 1905. Note the measurements for one are shown in inches, while the other is described in feet and inches.

No. 27 Wardrobe

Plain Oak. Gloss Finish.
7 ft. 5 in. high. 48 in. wide. 17 in. deep.
Extreme width 52 in.
12 x 48 British Bevel Mirror.

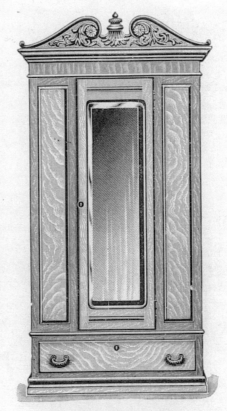

No. 121 Wardrobe

Plain Oak.
Mirror 14 x 48 British Bevel. Height 7 ft. 5 in.
Width Body 3 ft. 6 in.
Extreme width 3 ft. 11 in.
Depth 1 ft. 6 in. Shipped knocked down.
Easily put together. Finish—Golden polished.

No. 134 Library Bookcase

Height 59 in.   Width 28 in.   Glass Door.
Quarter Sawed Golden Oak
Finish—Polished.

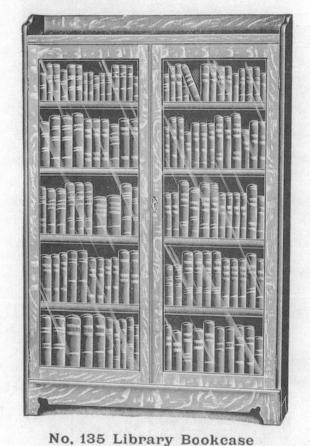

No. 135 Library Bookcase

Height 59 in.   Width 40 in.   Glass Doors.
Quarter Sawed Golden Oak.
Finish—Polished.

Library bookcases with glass doors, 1905.

A bed couch with
mattress No. 34, 1907.

No. 34 Bed Couch

Hard edge.   28 in. wide, 6 ft. 3 in. long.   With mattress.
When open, width, 4 ft. 10 in.
Grade, tapestry, No. 35.
Weight, 70 lbs.

$18.00   See price list for assorted

PRICE LIST

KRUG BROS. & CO.

WHOLESALE

Furniture • Manufacturers.

Chesley, Ontario.
1896.

No. 75 Five Piece Parlor Suite

Spring seat.
Hard edge.
Grade A, velour.
Weight, 130 lbs.

$35.00

See price-list for assorted coverings.

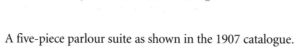

A five-piece parlour suite as shown in the 1907 catalogue.

CHAPTER 6

The Main Street Plant

As the demand for furniture grew in the western part of the country, the Krug brothers saw the necessity of being close to a railway for shipping. They investigated the possibility of having a spur line run down to the factory in the Saugeen River valley but this did not prove to be practical.

The established Chesley Rake & Novelty Company, which manufactured farm rakes, wooden knobs, potato mashers, rolling pins and other such utensils from scrap wood from the planing mill, had a two-storey brick factory on Main Street close to the local railway line. Krug Bros. purchased this company around 1900 and prepared to move operations to this new location. The roof of this building was raised to allow for a third storey. Other additions were made, including one in 1902 that measured 60 feet by 40 feet. While the main operations were still being carried on at the river factory, some work began in the so-called "Novelty Plant" with George Krug in charge.

In 1908, another addition, measuring 150 feet by 45 feet, was made to this new plant. This was the No. 3 building extending in a southerly direction from the office on Main Street. The contract for erecting this building, given to local builders, Mssrs. Henry Emke and Harry Lorenz,

The Novelty factory, located on Main Street in Chesley, was purchased by Krug Bros. circa 1900. The new Krug factory included this renovated brick structure, with an extension running north along Main Street, and ultimately west on King to Long Street.

called for the stonework to be done for 50 cents per perch (30 sq. yds.) and the brickwork for $3.50 per thousand. The inside walls were to be finished with one coat of plaster, included in the foregoing price. The stones, brick, sand and water were to be supplied by the furniture company, with the contractors supplying the balance of the requirements.

Two years later, in 1910, the building running from Main Street west along King Street was constructed. Here the office, the showroom and the warehouse and shipping departments were housed. This new structure was designated as buildings No. 1 and No. 2. It is interesting to

Krug employees based at the Novelty plant in 1901. George Krug, wearing a bowler hat, is standing in the doorway.

Three generations of the Witzke family: Peter (grandfather), Herb (father) and Larry (son), all working for the Krugs. This is but one example of multi-generations of families, all dedicated craftsmen, photo circa 1965.

note that part of the stone foundation, especially at the office end, was made from material that came from the stonework that had supported pillars for the first bridge of the Grand Trunk Railway built over the north branch of the Saugeen River. This limestone had originally come from a quarry on the xith Concession of Elderslie township.

In order to make room for these new factory buildings, three brick residences, situated along King Street, had to be removed. Instead of razing these houses, as would likely be done nowadays, the movers were called in. The three dwellings were shifted on rollers to their new

locations at 14 Division Street, 243 Main Street S., and 279 Main Street S. and became occupied immediately by the families of Steve Strba, Murhle Martin and Basil Ruhl, respectively.

Once the factory buildings were completed, management was able to move all the machinery and operations to the new site. This move was completed the following winter when it was easier to load and move machinery by sleigh. The Grand Trunk Railway ran a new switch into the shipping department so that the product could be loaded directly into railway cars. It was now very convenient for shipping a large amount of furniture to Western Canada, an area which was rapidly being settled. As there had already been a spur line running into the yard for delivering lumber and coal, now both incoming supplies and outgoing furniture could be shipped by rail.

The original dry kiln was a large frame building west of the boiler room. It was later used for veneer storage. In 1915, a new kiln was built with seven compartments, south of the factory along Main Street. These compartments were natural circulation kilns using the "Grand Rapids System" of drying. Fans situated under the stacks of lumber circulated hot air up and around the wood. As it took about a month to dry lumber this way, in 1950 the decision was

made to convert two of the compartments to the "Moore" type of forced circulation drying, which afforded better control over the drying process. A third was retained using the natural drying system and the other four were converted to storage compartments for dried lumber.

When the buildings were first built, an alleyway was left between the office and the No. 3 building on Main Street to allow vehicular access into the yard. As this was found to be of little use, it was bricked in a few years later.

After moving to the Main and King streets location, the upholstery department was located on the bottom floor of what was known as the No. 5 building. As a large amount of upholstered furniture, especially couches, was being made at this time, a track was run from the northwest corner of the building to the shipping room so that finished pieces could be transported by a four-wheeled push car. With the introduction of walnut-veneered furniture around 1920, space had to be found for the veneer department. When upholstery was moved to the second floor, veneer took its place on the first floor. The first foreman in charge of the veneer department is unknown, but John Graper moved from the machine department to be assistant foreman and later took over the responsibility of veneer until he was promoted to take charge of the

machine department when Jake Turrel retired in April 1953.

In 1926, a small addition of 40 feet by 20 feet was made to the building known as No. 7 to make more room in the breakout area of the first floor. It also allowed for more warehouse space in the second and third floors.

Management sought to reduce the high cost of fire insurance by installing a sprinkler system throughout the factory in 1926.

The Main Street factory and office building as it looked in the 1950s. The photo was taken by Jim Siegrist, nephew of Bruce Krug. His father, Al Siegrist, was married to Lily Krug and was a salesman for Krug Bros.

The entrance to the showroom for the Krug Bros. furniture, displaying pieces of solid cherry furniture, circa 1970s.

Contractor, H. S. Downer from Midland was hired for the job. The water tower, including a cypress tank with a capacity of 40,00 gallons, was added the following year. The wooden tank lasted until 1951 when it was replaced by a steel tank made by Hunter Bridge & Boiler Co. of Kincardine at a cost of $4,097.

In April 1927, a freak windstorm coming from the southwest struck the west end of No. 5 and No. 6, the south end of the building. The walls of the third storey were pushed in. The roof lifted and pieces scattered on the main street and neighbouring properties. The sprinkler pipes were broken and both finished furniture and stock-in-process were water damaged before the valves could be shut off. All employees were put to work the next day cleaning up the mess and repairing the building. Fred Shuknecht, a former mason working in the Finishing Department was in charge of the necessary brickwork. Martin Schilling and other cabinetmakers were drawn from the assembly department to replace the roof. In a few days the building was repaired and operations were back to normal. Later that year, Charlie Lettau tied members of the roof structure throughout the factory with heavy wire running down to the second floor to prevent a possible recurrence of the damage.

The Bruce Woodworkers Plant, formerly the Canada Beds Ltd., was purchased from the Town of Chesley in 1936, just before it was to be sold to the wreckers and demolished. This business had failed during the Depression and the property had reverted to the Town for non-payment of taxes. It was hoped that the building might provide a home for a future industry wishing to locate in Chesley. After being used for storage of wool from Australia during the early 1940s, it eventually found a use as a warehouse for veneer and surplus equipment.

After the CNR stopped using the railway freight shed, Krug Bros. leased it for storage purposes until 1974 when it was purchased. It proved an excellent place for storing cartons and veneer.

The factory, as seen from the rear, provides a clear view of the steel tank water tower erected in 1951 to replace the original wooden tank. The cone-shaped structure sucked the fine wood dust through the pipe for disposal in the boiler room furnace. This 100-foot chimney stack was used as a familiar navigation guide for WWII pilots-in-training. The water tower still stands, but the factory buildings are gone.

CHAPTER 7

The Production of Lumber

Lumber is the principal raw material used for manufacturing furniture. Soon after the business was started, the Krugs decided to install a small sawmill to produce lumber from the plentiful supply of standing hardwood in the area. It is believed that the first sawmill was housed in the former felt mill on the south side of the river, which the Krugs had purchased from Rolston. Sometime early in the twentieth century that building was replaced by a second mill building with a tramway running out of the west end. The tramway ran across the river, along the north side, beyond the railroad bridge and onto property leased from William Elliot. The lumber, which had been pushed down the track on a four-wheeled car, was off-loaded and piled.

After the factory operations were moved to the plant at Main and King streets in 1911, a switch was built on this tramway near the railroad bridge and a track built in the opposite direction to allow lumber to be piled on the north side of the river.

In the earlier years the logs were usually delivered to the mill by horse-drawn sleighs in the winter. River driving was attempted with logs being delivered to the river at various places between vith Concession of Sullivan and the

A line-up of horse-drawn wagons at the Krug sawmill in Chesley, ready to be hitched to the teams of horses.

town line. However, the loss of hardwood logs through sinking was too great and river driving was discontinued.

The stock of logs brought in by sleighs would usually last until the summer when mill operations would cease until sleighing began again in the early winter. One year, the mill operated day and night because there were so many logs to saw before they spoiled with the summer heat. This was the year after the Good Friday windstorm of March 21, 1913.

In 1899, a farm with standing timber on it was purchased at Kinghurst in Sullivan township, ten miles east of Chesley. Several other properties close by were acquired until 600 acres were assembled. As there was a large amount of standing timber in that area, it became necessary to purchase another sawmill. The Moore sawmill at Mooresburg, bought for $2,000 in 1904, was moved to Kinghurst so that logs could be sawn closer to their origin and then hauled as lumber to Chesley. The deal included the logs in the mill yard and Lot 24, Concession III, Sullivan township. This lot was covered with standing timber at that time.

A steam engine was used to develop the power for the mill. Two HRT boilers fired with waste wood generated the steam. The operation here, as in most mills in that time, was seasonal.

It ran from breakup in the spring until early summer when all the logs would have been sawn. This mill continued each year until about 1918. After that, logs cut or purchased in the Kinghurst area were trucked to the Chesley mill. John Krug was in charge of the Kinghurst operation and, for at least one season, acted as head sawyer. Other head sawyers included Ed Galbraith, Mike Schilling and Charlie Lettau.

For several years the men working in the company bush were housed in a log shanty. Later, a frame building was centrally located on the property so that little time was lost going to and coming from work. The frame shanty was later converted into the maple syrup evaporator house.

Around the beginning of the twentieth century, a large number of logs were being brought in from the area about six miles north of Kinghurst. Rough and hilly land, it was actually an area of rubble left by a post-glacial moraine. With stories of the ruggedness of the terrain of the Klondike in the Yukon being prominent in the minds of Canadians at that time period, the locals gave the area the nickname, "The Klondike," a name which has stuck to this day.

While the mill was operating, there were three residences on the company property at

To the left is the original Krug factory beside the Krug dam. Next is the sawmill. Note the ramp with a rail carriageway. Behind the sawmill is the stable for the teams of horses. The factory to the right housed the office and the finishing and upholstering departments. Behind is the original Chesley school, circa 1910.

Kinghurst. The main house, which was occupied by the foreman, also served as a boarding house for some of the employees. The other two frame houses were situated farther north along the VITH Concession. The house closest to the mill was occupied by the fireman so that he was readily available to look after the boilers.

When the sawmill at Kinghurst ceased to operate, the machinery was removed and the building was used in the winter to house some of a large flock of sheep which pastured on the open land in the summer. After the sheep were sold, around 1929, the building was taken down.

The coming of the automobile brought a change to the way logs were transported. By 1918, logs were being purchased for truck delivery in the summer. The sawmill operation was no longer dependent on winter delivery only. Now it could function through the summer for as long as logs were available. Trucking also meant that logs farther away could be purchased. However, such transport could be carried out only while the roads were open. Effectively, this meant that up until 1932, no logs were trucked during the winter. Remarkably, that winter there was very little snow and Earl Rushton started hauling logs from a bushlot in "The Klondike" which he and George McCurdy were cutting. Logs were still brought in by sleigh whenever the snow conditions were suitable. Once snowplows began snow removal on the roads, sleigh transportation of logs ended.

The Chesley sawmill operated until February 20, 1940, when it was destroyed by fire believed to have been caused by faulty wiring. The mill was equipped with a log jack, power nigger (a machine covered with spikes which turned the logs), log carriage, husk and head saw, edger, slab saw and shingle saw. The latter was used for cutting drawer-side material from heavy slabs. All this machinery was belt-driven by the power generated from the river with a Barber 60-inch horizontal turbine or

The Chesley sawmill in the spring of 1967. By now, all that is left of the original factory site are the sawmill and a section of the upholstery building. There is a new bridge over the Saugeen, and a new school has replaced the former one that burned about 1948.

waterwheel.

The sawmill of the Southampton Lumber Co., situated on the south side of the mouth of the Saugeen River, was purchased in the spring of 1940 to replace the burned Krug mill. Hector Diebel of Allenford was given the contract of dismantling it, moving the structure to Chesley, and re-erecting it — with some modifications — at the site of the previous mill. The Krug mill foreman, George Hepburn, and Ernest Lueck, who had previous experience in setting up sawmills, were in charge of the installation of the machinery and equipment. By late August the mill was operating, using water power from the dam which had not been seriously damaged by the fire.

Two logs from John McDonald, a farmer and conservationist living near Tara, 1943.

The International Motor Trucks catalogues of 1920 carried a range of testimonials from owners. The Krug Bros. endorse their Model 101 International Truck. "We have used this truck principally for hauling logs a distance of nine miles from our sawmill. In spite of the hilly nature of the country and the rough roads, we are hauling as many logs with one truck as would ordinarily take twenty teams." International Model 101 - maximum capacity 10, 000 pounds. Some specifications: Tire Equipment: solid only; Engine: 4 cylinder block cast;...engine in front of radiator, easily accessible; Clutch: dry plate multiple disk, asbestos lined; Gasoline Capacity: 18 gallon tank in cowl; Regular Equipment: front fenders, oil tail lamp, 2 gas head lamps, Prest-O-Lite tank, horn and tools.

When the mill at Chesley was rebuilt in 1940, it operated on a year-round basis except for brief shutdowns for maintenance or when low water necessitated shorter working hours. George Hepburn was the foreman in charge from 1927 until his death in 1970. (Earlier foremen were Werner Pommer Sr. and Charlie Lettau.) Walter McDonald carried on for four years, followed by John Dirstein, who worked until the mill was destroyed by fire on the cold winter night of January 24, 1975.

A team of horses was used in the Chesley mill yard for skidding logs, hauling out the lumber and slabs, and taking the sawdust to the

factory. Some of the teamsters over the years were Ernst Borkholst, Sam Curtis, William Priebe, John Heldt, Henry Haug, Steve Dustow, Ken Klages and Edgar Struke. In 1959, the use of horses was discontinued and a Massey Ferguson Work Bull tractor, purchased for $3,773, was used for mill yard work. Hauling lumber to the factory was done by truck.

The first truck used for transporting logs was a Brantford chain drive purchased in 1919. Over the years, however, management favoured International trucks. In 1957, to facilitate the loading of logs, a Heab crane was added to the trucks. Since then it has been demonstrated that a log truck equipped with a crane for loading was a saving of energy as no additional power was required to move logs. Drivers of the Krug log trucks included George Hepburn, Archie McDonald, Sam Hepburn, Ed Yule, Walter McDonald, Ed Albright, Fred Fortune and Louis Albright.

The logs were hauled into the mill in a low four-wheeled truck, which brought them from the river when the water levels were adequate in the summer. If the water was too low in the summer or the pond was frozen in the winter, the logs had to be rolled from a log deck on land.

In 1976, the sawmill machinery at the RCA plant in Owen Sound was purchased with the intention of installing it in a new mill. It was to be built in the factory yard where the night watchman could keep an eye on it and prevent a repeat of the 1940 fire and the later 1975 one. Various factors prevented the carrying out of this project.

Purchased logs or those cut from the Krug tree farms have been sawn for a time by Jerry McGlynn at his portable mill which he moved into the yard. At other times Zooks Custom Mill,

Bruce Krug (left) and Howard, with sawyer Ed Derbecker examining the giant "Krug Elm" in the Kinghurst Tract in 1973. Many tree buffs and media people came to witness the removal of this huge elm tree, dead of Dutch elm disease. At the time it was the largest, forest-grown elm hardwood tree in Canada. Its diameter at breast height was 58″ and its board foot volume was 4000 feet. Ring growth indicated its age as 305 years. The Krugs estimated that the tree would yield enough material to manufacture 20 solid elm bedroom suites. *Photo by James Seigrist, Krug Collection.*

Krug Bros. employees pose around a tractor purchased to replace the teams of horses. By this time it was hard to find anyone who would work as a teamster and care for the horses. From left to right: George Hepburn, Sam Hepburn, Walter McDonald, unidentified, Edgar Struke, George Kincaid, Bill Molson, Jack Specht, Dave Busch; in front: Gerald Reilly, leaning against rear tractor tire, Ed Smith, Ed Yule. *Photo by James Siegrist in 1958, from Bruce Krug Collection.*

three miles west of Chesley, carried out the sawing.

The Chesley sawmill continued to function until 1975, at which point the equipment was dismantled and, for the first time since its early settlement, Chesley no longer had a mill.

Employees at Krug Bros. sawmill in Chesley, May 1958. Back Row (from l to r): Jack Specht, Dave Busch, George Kincaid, Bill Molson, Ed Yule; front: George Hepburn, Ed Smith, Edgar Struke, Gerald Reilly, Sam Hepburn, Nelson Wedaw, Walter McDonald. *Photo by James Siegrist, 1958, from Bruce Krug Collection.*

CHAPTER 8

The Maple Syrup Operation

In 1917, when the sawmill was still operating at Kinghurst, the directors of the company decided that some additional revenue could be found by starting a maple syrup operation. The 400-acre tract of mostly maple trees just east of the mill would provide their base.

In preparation for start-up in the spring of 1918, a Grimm evaporator and all the necessary equipment was purchased. A frame building, formerly used as a logging camp to accommodate the men working in the bush, was converted to house the evaporator and canning room. John Krug, the eldest brother, was in charge of the operation with Charlie Lettau as foreman. In this first year, there had not been much wood prepared for boiling the sap so old log buildings, the remains of an former logging camp at the site, were cut up and used.

The first year's trial must have been successful as more and more sap buckets were purchased — until it ultimately became a 2800-bucket operation. In the spring of 1919, the Department of Agriculture sent up a movie crew to film the work. This film was included with footage from of two other operations in the province for publicity purposes. With the syrup operation now firmly established, there was a noticeable change in the management of the woods. Significantly, only trees starting to spoil were harvested for logs and fuel wood.

About 1921, Charlie Lettau moved to Chesley and Sam Hepburn took over as foreman. He carried on until 1929 when he became the postmaster at Desboro and was replaced by Harvey Sulkye. About this time, because of the illness of John Krug, Howard Krug, Christian's oldest son, assumed responsibility for this enterprise.

At the peak of operations, there were usually five men employed, two at the syrup

Gathering sap at Kinghurst, circa 1942.

The marketing label for the Krug Bros. maple syrup - Saugeen Pure Maple Syrup. The production of maple syrup was discontinued in 1963.

house and three gathering sap. This extra help was supplied by neighbouring farmers and their sons who were pleased to earn supplementary pay during their off-season. On weekends many visitors would walk down the road for almost a mile, intent on venturing into the sugar bush to see syrup being made and to sample the product.

Early in the summer of 1951, there was a bad outbreak of forest tree tent caterpillar and the hardwood trees were nearly all defoliated. This was followed in June 1952 by another severe tent caterpillar defoliation. With no leaves maturing for two years in a row, the decision was made for the coming year, 1953, to drop syrup making in order to give the trees a chance to recover.

This recovery period stretched into five years and syrup was not made again until 1958. Sam Hepburn, who by now was driving the company's log truck and living in Chesley, took over as foreman. By this time many of the buckets had deteriorated so the operation was, of necessity, much smaller. Only 600 buckets were put out annually in 1958 and 1959.

Late in the 1950s, a new system of gathering sap with plastic tubing and pipelines came into use. The old syrup building was disintegrating so a new evaporator house was built in 1959 at the west end of the bush, constructed in such a way to make use of the slope of the hills. Pipes and tubing lines were laid out so that the sap would run straight to the syrup house by gravity. Here, a new 5 feet by 15 feet Grimm evaporator was installed. In addition, a power line was connected to the site from the farm buildings in order to supply electricity for lights and for the vacuum pump which evacuated the sap lines.

About 1000 taps were put out to feed the evaporator. Future plans included tapping trees over a wider area of the bush on the east side of the hill. In reality, 1000 taps were not enough to keep the evaporator going. This additional sap would have been either transported or pumped to the evaporator. However, it was found that even with the new system and equipment, the syrup operation was a marginal one at best. It was decided not to increase the scope of the existing enterprise.

Syrup was made at this new evaporator house for three years, from 1960 to 1963. That was the year that Sam Hepburn retired and the maple syrup business was temporarily discontinued until proper help could be found, with a permanent employee living in the farmhouse. Sadly, the desired type of worker was unavailable. Ultimately it became necessary to close down and dispose of the evaporator and other equipment. In 1980, Carman Hodgson purchased and moved the equipment to Keppel township to operate under the name, "Georgian Bay Maples Inc.," unfortunately no longer in existence.

A recent winter view of the sugar shack at Kinghurst. *Photo courtesy Telfer Wegg.*

CHAPTER 9

Woodlots and Tree Farms

Around 1900, the company purchased 500 acres of land, Lot 27, Concession IV and Concession V; and the east half of Lot 28, Concession V at Kinghurst. Another 100 acres was bought at near-by Harrison Lake, at the north half of Lot 26, Concession IV. These properties were covered with good standing hardwood. Krug Bros. also purchased the Moore sawmill at Mooresburg and moved it to Kinghurst, about five miles east of its original site.

At that time the intention was to completely log these well-wooded areas for their furniture manufacturing, but over the years they were actually selectively logged. About 75% of mature timber was always left standing. The Krugs came to the realization that trees were a finite resource. Once a tree was cut, it was gone. Therefore, the continuing need for a source of wood to produce furniture would have to be met with an intelligent plan for the use of available woodlots. Selective rather than clear cuttings became their watchword. Aside from this practical consideration, they knew that over-logging led to fire. The Bruce Peninsula after being almost completely logged-over in the first 40 years of the 19th century and the first decade of the 20th century, was subject to devastating fire.

Whenever lightning caught the deserts of slash, discarded branches and wood chips left after squaring timber and tangles of windfalls, they made up a veritable tinderbox.

Several years ago the Kinghurst Tract was described by a prominent forester as being a unique forested property in southern Ontario. At the time of purchase, the property was described as the "Kinghurst Bush." The name came from the hamlet of Kinghurst which in turn had received its name from the King family. It has been the base from which it and various other properties were developed into the company's present-day tree farms.

As farming was carried on at the Kinghurst properties with the pasturing of cattle and sheep, new growth of trees on the open lands did not succeed. In 1929, the Murray Tract of 150 acres — the north quarter of Lot 30 and south half of Lot 29, Concession VI, Sullivan township, was purchased from Dugald Murray. It consisted of 100 acres of cedar swamp and upland hardwood, with the balance in former agricultural land. Since this property was fenced, there was now an opportunity for potential reforestation. The Forestry Branch of the Ontario Department of Lands and Forests was then promoting the replenishing of forests. Trees were supplied at no charge, except for the delivery freight. They were to be suitably planted and protected. An area at the east end of the property was selected and around 3,000 trees were ordered for the spring planting of 1931 to take place under the supervision of Howard Krug. These were planted around the end of April in furrows ploughed by Bert King and his team of horses. Sam Hepburn, Percy Moss, Millard Liebeck and Archie Harvie assisted in the planting.

Red pine was the principal species of tree used. Howard Krug chose this variety because, as a forestry student in 1924, he had visited the red pine plantation at the St. William Provincial Nursery near Lake Erie and had been mightily impressed. There was also a scattering of white pine and some experimental hardwoods. As red oak is a common tree in the area and as it grows farther north, east and south in Ontario, it was decided to try some. Since this area is close to the northern limit of the natural range of black walnut, some of that species was also planted. A large amount of walnut lumber was being used in the factory at this time; all of it imported from the United States. Older members of the firm in particular, liked the idea of growing their own supply of lumber, especially the black walnut. Earlier, it had been noted on a purchase of soft maple logs, that the annual growth rings were

Timber resources managed by Krug Bros. *Photo courtesy Telfer Wegg.*

were also ordered to see what might develop.

At first, the red oak of the 1931 planting appeared to be a failure. Grasshoppers took a liking to the leaves and, for several years, the foliage was mostly eaten off. However, eventually some of the trees survived and by 1995 there were several specimens with a DBH (diameter at breast height) of 12 inches. Late spring frosts were hard on the walnuts — freezing the buds back, year after year. In a more sheltered area of the tree plantation — the southeast corner — the walnuts did better. The trees there, in 1995, measured 17 inches DBH, while other walnuts scattered throughout the plantation were just 14 to 15 inches DBH. The soft maples, however, were mostly a failure, just growing up as bushy shrubs. At first it was thought that the Carolina poplar planting was also unsuccessful, but a scattering of them (1995) were found at around 14 inches DBH. One of the Carolina poplars, planted at the Krug cottage in Port Elgin near Izzard Street, had phenomenal growth and, in 1995 measured 56 inches DBH. Although the plantation was not the best site for red pine, they have done quite well with many now exceeding the 14 inches DBH class.

To show that furniture can be made from trees after only 27 years of growth, Sam Hepburn who was back working for the

running between ¼ and ⅜ inches, indicating a good rate of growth — so some soft maple seedlings were selected to be put in at the same time. In addition, fifty Carolina poplar cuttings

company, cut four of the red pine in 1958. They were sawn into 1-inch lumber at the sawmill and, after kiln drying, were used to make a desk in "Plantation Pine." This desk had a place in the showroom for many years and today is included in the "Krug Collection of Furniture" in the Bruce County Museum at Southampton.

After the successful start of tree planting in 1931, a total of 2,000 more red pine were ordered for planting in 1932. They were set in the southeast corner of the Murray Tract. A field a little farther to the west was the next to be reforested. At the northeast corner of the Tract there was a gravelly hill where jack pine were planted. During the next few years, other parts of the Murray Tract and some small areas at Kinghurst were selected for reforestation. Throughout, red pine was the favoured species, along with a scattering of white pine, white spruce and walnut.

Most farming activity on the Kinghurst properties had been discontinued by the mid-1930s. The Harrison Lake section of the property, with about 30 acres of marginal land at the east end, was selected for the next additional planting. About 1000 trees, predominantly red pine, were planted here. It was decided to plant the rest of the tract over a period of about three years, depending on time available in the spring.

Again, red pine seedlings were ordered in advance. However, John Jackson, the forester supervising activity in this area for the Department of Lands and Forests, reported an infestation of the pine-shoot moth in some parts of the province. He advised against planting pure red pine. As it was too late to order white pine, he suggested planting the red pine in rows 12 to 14 feet apart and then planting alternate rows of white pine the following year. This advice was followed and the infestation of the shoot moth did not occur. This was the first planting done with a planting machine on any of the company properties.

Because of the nature of the soil and dry weather during planting, there was considerable mortality in this two-year planting. In the following year, trees were ordered to fill in the open spaces as well as for the balance of the land. Scotch pine Christmas tree plantations were proliferating and, as this appeared to be an opportunity for an early financial return, some of this species was ordered along with the red and white pine. When the trees were delivered, the three varieties were found to be thoroughly mixed-up, which made the special care necessary for developing Christmas trees uneconomical. Actually, the Scotch pine have, for the most part, done poorly. This, however, is fortuitous because the space is being taken over by the healthy red and white pines.

Ren Milburn of Desboro was holding a 40 acre property of hardwood in the Klondike area of Sullivan township — part of Lot 12, Concession vi — which his family had owned since the time they had operated a sawmill at Desboro. When this property came up for sale in 1941, a deal was made whereby the Krug company purchased the east 35 acres for $4,000. At the time of purchase, the property was assessed at three hundred dollars. In the two successive years the assessment was raised first to $400 and then $500. No complaint was made so the Township assessor raised the assessment to $1,500 the next year! This property, still in Krug ownership, is now termed the "Klondike Tract" of the Krug Tree Farms.

Frank Twalmley, a farmer, living at Lot 30, Concession viii, Bentinck township, owned a lot across the road. It had a nice hardwood area of about ten acres at the south end, and a cedar swamp bordering a mud lake at the northeast part. The remainder was mainly marginal farmland. In 1943, the company purchased this piece of land for $3,500. The open land was rented to neighbouring farmers for several years until, in 1981, the Woodlot Improvement Act (WIA) agreement #83-697G was signed with the Ministry of Natural Resources to have this open land planted with trees. Most were to be machine planted. However, since some of the land had never been cultivated, it was too rough for the machine and had to be hand planted. Here, white pine was the favoured species, but some red pine and white spruce were also used. In 1969, when the elms were dying, those still living were logged and in 1982 a cut was taken from the hardwood area. Unfortunately, when the scattered elm in the cedar swamp died, the water table rose, tree roots were loosened and winds blew down most of the cedar.

Three bachelor brothers, John, Dan and William Wade lived together at Lot 14, Concession ii WGR, Bentinck township. Together they held 400 acres (Lots 11, 12, 13, 14); John owned 150 acres, Dan 150 and William the remaining land of 100 acres. When John and Dan both died, William was not capable of carrying on alone. The block of land came up for sale by tender through the Bruce and Grey Trust Company in the summer of 1943. The Trust Company had its own peculiar way of more or less privately auctioning a property after it had selected the highest bids and then working the highest bidders against each other. Experiences with previous properties auctioned in this way in which the company had lost out, and the tenacity with which Ephraim Krause of Williamsford (who favoured the purchase by Krug Bros.) stuck to the deal, resulted in the purchase of all four lots by Krug for $7,700. Later, it was decided to sell the farmland and buildings to Wilfred Monk and retain an area of 142 acres at the east end of the tract that contained most of the woodland. This consisted of mostly hardwood with about 30 acres of clear land at the southwest corner and about 40 acres of cedar swamp. Part of this swamp, on Lot 11, is an example of typical virgin or climax cedar swamp, with some of the largest cedar in Canada, along with spruce and occasional white pine. It was described by the late Robert Mortley, a long-time resident of the Dornoch area, as woodland that had never seen an axe. While it is not heavily timbered, some of the large cedars are still green today. Others are dead, but either still standing or down. There is no evidence of fire having gone through it leaving charred stumps as in the continuing swamp to the south in Lots 12 and 13.

Thirty acres of clear land on the former Wade lots were planted in mostly white pine with some red pine and white spruce. These trees have grown very well and, in 1981, under the WIA agreement #83-689G, the Ministry of Natural Resources arranged to have the crop trees selected and pruned. This whole tract, now known as the Wade Tract of the Krug Tree Farms, is a valued section of the Krug holdings.

In 1952, a property of 100 acres, Lot 8, Concession II WGR, Bentinck township in Grey County, belonging to the Stewart Estate, came up for sale by tender and, once more, the company's bid was successful. This tract consists of about ten acres of hardwood at the east end, some soft maple, elm, cedar in the low land at the west end, and about 60 acres in between of open land and cedar regeneration. The open land has been planted with white and red pine and occasional black walnut. This has been a successful planting except that, in the areas where there was a considerable amount of natural regeneration of cedar, a large percentage of the white pines was killed by rabbits.

In 1957, the Egremont Tract in Bruce County of 49 acres (west 1/2 of Lot 8, Concession II EGR) was purchased. This was completely covered by a natural woodland that had been conservatively logged over the years and retained a nice, growing stand of hard maple. In 1969, as the elms were beginning to be infected by Dutch elm disease, some 25,000 feet were cut by Wilfred Monk. Sadly, while he was cutting an elm, it jumped the stump and pinned him against an adjacent tree and he was killed.

During 1985 to 1986, because of pressure from the bank to reduce the business loan, it was decided to sell this property to the Klemmer Lumber Co. of Lamlash, a hamlet northeast of Hanover.

For some time, Lot 5, Concession IV, Amabel township was the property of the Wylie family. It had about 18 acres of good hardwood at the north end — mostly of maple and beech. When it came up for sale after Mr. Wylie's death, Krug Bros. purchased it. Most of it was good agricultural land that the company severed and sold, while keeping the woodlot section. These 18 acres of hardwood comprise the Parkhead Tract of the Krug Tree Farms which today still stands intact.

The Arran Lake Tract, part of Lots 6 and 7, Concession IX, Arran township, was purchased by tender from the McIntosh Estate in 1967. It consists of about 94 acres, as the balance of the two lots is part of Arran Lake. Here was a hardwood tract of maple, elm and beech in 25 acres extending from the road to the west side of the lake, with farmland to the north and south of the bush. As the elm had already been infected with the Dutch elm disease, a contract was given to the nearby Maes brothers to log whatever elm was salvageable. They cut 112,000 feet during the following two winters. Today the tract still stands with its extensive forest of maple and beech.

Besides the tree farms, over the years the company purchased various other properties for the woodlots. Three of these were held for quite a number of years. Before World War I, property that would have been flooded by a dam planned by the Krug Bros. at Lot 27, Concession II, Elderslie township, was acquired by the company. Most of the log trees here were cut in 1912 and 1917. Except for the area sold to the Town of Chesley for sewage lagoons, this property has been held intact and parts have grown up in natural regeneration.

In 1920, a farm on the XTH Concession of Brant township (Lot 10, Con XI and part of Lot 10, Con X) came up for sale after the death of John Watson, a pioneer settler who had taken up the land from the Crown in the mid-19th century. There were about 20 acres of bush at the north end that have been logged by the company at various times. One of the heavier cuts was in 1933-35 when about 40,000 feet were taken out. Many of the smaller maples were cut for fuel as they had died during the severe winter weather of February, 1933 when the temperature dipped to minus 40 degrees Fahrenheit. Most of the farm is agricultural land and has been rented over the years for farm purposes.

Henry Berry and his sister lived on the farm

that their father held before them at Lot 34, Concessions VII and VIII, Brant township. After Henry died, the 160-acre property was purchased since there was a good hardwood woodlot across the west end of the farm. As the property was mainly farmland, it was rented out with the tenants occupying the house until the building was destroyed by fire. Over the years, some of the tenants helped to pay their rent by cutting logs. About 63,000 feet was taken out this way. Donald Ahrens cut most of the logs during the years 1973, 1974 and 1983. As there was gravel in the hills of this farm, the property was sold to Township of Brant in 1986 as a source of gravel for the township roads.

The Krug Tree Farms, as they are now called, include those described, as well as various properties purchased by Bruce and Howard Krug for forestry purposes. In 1933, a 60-acre property, part of Lots 23 and 24, Concession IV, Sullivan township, was offered to the company by Robert McClung, in order to clear up a title. As the company decided that there was insufficient timber on it, Howard Krug purchased it personally. The open land was planted during the years 1961 to 1962 by Saugeen Valley Conservation Authority crews with a total of 40,000 trees. This property today displays the results of that reforestation about forty years ago.

Another property in Grey County, a 79-acre property at Lot 15, Concession IX EGR, Holland township, belonging to the Hamilton Bros. of Holland Centre, was purchased in 1941. The Hamiltons had a water-powered sawmill in Holland township (the farthest upstream of all the power dams on the north branch of the Saugeen River). The lot was acquired by Eph Krause of Williamsford and Howard Krug. The Hamilton Bros. had liberally logged it about 25 years before and now it was partly swamp, along with a mixture of second growth and old growth hardwood. In 1946, Eph Krause sold his interest to Howard Krug. Today, the parcel of land is called the Lily Oak Tract of the Krug Tree Farms after the nearby community and school.

Two properties purchased by Bruce Krug are included in the Tree Farms. The first is Lot 56, Concession II NCD, Amabel township purchased in 1955. This is completely wooded, consisting of white pine at the north end and a variety of cedar, balsam, spruce, poplar and white birch over the remainder of the land. Known as the Amabel Tract, this tree farm is still intact today.

His second property is in Lindsay township at Lot 14, Concession VI WBR, also purchased in 1955. An option had been taken on this property so that it could be added to the Bruce County Miller Lake Forest, but when the Township of Lindsay decided against having any more County Forest in the township, Bruce picked up the option. At various times, the property had been totally burnt over and, at the time of purchase, was covered with second growth red cedar, spruce, balsam, poplar and white birch, a combination which makes it a good hunting area. Over the last forty plus years, the timber has grown considerably.

The Maluske Tract of 32 acres, purchased in 1957, is the smallest of the tree farms. Located in the west part of the north 1/2 of Lot 20, Concession VIII, Sullivan township of Grey County, it is mainly hard maple and beech, with some soft maple at the west end. This was purchased as a 100-acre property but the house, barn and 68 acres have been severed and sold, with a right of way reserved to allow access to the woodlot. This property was sold some years ago.

Another 100-acre property in Grey County, Lot 9, Concession III EGR, Glenelg township was purchased in 1957 from Patrick Barry. Some of this land had been cleared and farmed, but had gone back into bush — except for two small fields. One of these fields was selected in 1957 to grow Scotch pine for Christmas trees. In 1981,

red cedars were planted in the gaps left after the Christmas trees were cut and continue to flourish today.

When the west half of Lot 30, Concession IX, Sullivan township was listed in a tax sale it was purchased by Bruce in 1957. Title was obtained in 1961 after the required four-year interval. Along with about 70 acres of open land, there was a 28-acre swamp and two acres of hardwood in the north-central area. The place was rented to neighbouring farmers for several years, but, in 1966, it was decided to have the open land planted the following year as a Centennial project. Once the WIA Agreement #83-308 was signed with the Ministry of Natural Resources, a three-year planting was established. The first part, south and west of the creek flowing diagonally across it, was planted in 1967. The southeast section was planted in 1968 and the northeast part the following year. Red and white pine with a small amount of white spruce were the chosen species. It was the white pine that ultimately made the best showing. A large part of the planting was done with a planting machine with very good results. This, the first planting in Grey County under the Woodlots Improvement Act of 1966, is known today as the Centennial Tract.

Archie Watson of St. Edmunds township in

Reforestation - planning timber for the future.

Bruce County had a small sawmill near Tobermory. He had purchased 500 acres at and near Umbrella Lake. Most of this area had been burnt over in previous years and had grown up with a scattered cover of pine, spruce, balsam, cedar, poplar and white birch. Some of these trees were large enough for a profitable cut. After he logged these larger trees in 1958, Watson sold the properties to Bruce and Howard Krug. The property was inexpensive and was purchased with the hope, that some day, barring more fires, it would again bear mature timber. This property, along with four tax-sale shore properties nearby, of about eight acres each, are included in the Umbrella Lake Tract. They are all within the boundary of Bruce Peninsula National Park, which was established in 1989.*

The Pedwell family had a large acreage of land in St. Edmunds township, parts of which they sold off at various times. In 1963, 1000 acres consisting of Lots 6 to 10, Concession i and ii WBR, came up for sale and were purchased. Later that year when the Pedwell family offered Lots 11 to 15 in the same concessions, these were also purchased by the brothers and became known as the Crane River Tract because of the stream that crosses the property. Later, Lots 7, 10 and the E 1/2 of 14 in the iiiRD Concession were added to this tree farm, making a total of about 2,240 acres. While most of this land has been burnt over in the past, there was quite good regeneration on much of it, although the Spruce budworm has played havoc with the spruce and balsam. An outstanding feature of this tract is a small area at the west end of Lots 10 and 11, Concession ii, where a scattering of virgin white and red pine trees still stand today. This is possibly the only group of such trees left on the Bruce Peninsula. Some of them show the telltale marks of fire, at the butts of the trees. Fresh bark grows only part way over fire scars, leaving a characteristic marking referred to as "cat faces." North of the Crane River on Lot 7, there is an acreage of mature hardwood that was either missed by the fires or covered by ground fire only, leaving no noticeable damage to the trees. In 1995, a cedar tree at the edge of the river measured 43 inches DBH, illustrating the size to which the trees of the Peninsula once grew.

The Pleasant Hill Tract consists of 150 acres, Lot 5 and N 1/2 Lot 6, Concession iii WGR, Bentinck township in Grey County. It was purchased from the Earl Grant Estate in 1960. The Christies who had a mill early in the twentieth century on Lot 30, Concession vii, Sullivan township, had logged the property some time earlier. Earl Grant had acquired it from the Christies about 1950 and had operated a portable sawmill there. Over the years, part of this property had been cleared and farmed by the Skene family. Their buildings had been at the top of the hill near the east end where there was such a nice view of the surrounding area that it was called "The Pleasant Hill Place" by the Christies. Most of the open land was planted with white pine and white spruce when Earl Grant owned the property. The balance was planted in 1964 with red pine, white pine and white spruce so that the whole property would be forested with either natural forest or planted forest, all of which stands today.

The Christie Estate also had a property of 49 acres at Lot 28, Concession xv, Bentinck township. In 1963, it too was purchased. This is all natural hardwood bush except for a pond of about three acres at the north end. Christies had a portable mill at the west side of the pond about 1920 when they took a cut of logs. Another cut was taken around 1940, and John Christie took another cut of 21,000 feet in 1961. When the Christie Tract was purchased in 1963, there was still some log lumber there, but it was mainly a growing bush requiring time to catch up. When Dutch elm disease began killing off all the elms, Willard Krouter was given the job of taking out whatever elms were large enough for logs. Some 18,000 feet were harvested in 1973.

The Derby Tract consists of 247 acres in the IIND Concession, being parts of Lots 4 and 5. The Sydenham River formed the west boundary. Part of this was purchased from Fred Cavell in 1955, and the balance of about 83 acres from the McNabb Estate in 1960. At this time there were about 100 acres of woodland with pastureland on the rest of the acreage. The wooded area consisted of about 25 acres of upland hardwood with the remainder being soft maple, elm and cedar with a small grove of swamp white oak. In 1976, the WIA Agreement #83-112G was signed with the Ministry of Natural Resources for the reforesting of the open land. Over the ensuing two years, white pine with some white spruce around the west end were planted on the property. Some girdling, cutting through the bark around the circumference of a tree, was carried out in the existing hardwood (maple and cherry) areas as an improvement measure. This was unfortunate, as these trees would have been more valuable a few years later as a fuel crop.

The north half of Lot 11, Concession ix, Brant township was purchased from William Bierworth of Hamilton in 1970. The Bierworth family had owned this land for many years. At that time, there were about 33 acres of natural hardwood with some log timber in the 50 to 60 year age class. It had been heavily logged in around 1929. The Bierworths had planted about five acres with Scotch pine, white spruce, walnut and black locust. About 15 acres at the south end were clear and this was planted in white pine in 1980 under WIA Agreement #83-625B.

The south 80 acres of Lot 31, Concession XIII, Brant township in Bruce County was mostly open pastureland. It had been purchased by Christian Krug in 1936, to be used in conjunction with the farm at Lot 30, Concession I, Elderslie township. In 1971, Bruce and Howard Krug bought it from the Christian Krug Estate with the idea of planting it to establish a memorial forest in memory of their parents — Christian Krug and Mary Hauser Krug. With the exception of a part at the south end, which was considered to be agricultural land, a WIA Agreement #40-2-55 was signed for the planting of all of the property. The Ministry of Natural Resources planted most of the agreement area in 1972. In the agricultural area, arrangements were made with the Saugeen Valley Conservation Authority to plant white pine and black walnut. This was carried out with a tree-planting machine in alternating rows of pine and walnut. Unfortunately, the furrows here were made too deep, and the resulting growth was poor with much of the pine and most of the walnut dying. In 1975, the WIA Agreement was

extended to include all of this area and spot planting was carried out to fill spaces caused by the high mortality. As these continue to grow to maturity, there will be a good mix of the two species.

The extensive, thoughtful woodlot management practised by the Krug family since the early years of the 20th century has resulted in an abundance of beautiful and valuable forests in both Bruce and Grey counties. In fact, whenever one encounters a well-wooded area in this area, it is usually safe to assume that it belongs to the Krug brothers. These forests provide an environment for wildlife, retain water table levels and protect the soil. Bruce Krug is also quick to point out the value of meadows and wetlands which, taken together with forest, protect the natural ecology of our lovely countryside.

* The Bruce Peninsula Natural Park, 136 square kilometres in size, protects a rugged limestone landscape and is one of the largest remaining tracts of forest in Southern Ontario.

CHAPTER 10

The Great Depression

The story of any business organization that existed through the 1930s would not be complete without mention of the trying times of that decade.

During the postwar years following WWI, business had been going along as usual and there was a good inventory of furniture in the factory warehouse in late 1929. Then the economy changed. As business fell off, the factory kept working full-time. Furniture was put into storage until the warehouse was crammed to the ceiling. Extra storage space was found wherever possible on the working floors of the factory. Urged on by his brothers, William made almost

weekly trips to Toronto to get what business he could. He became so familiar to the clerks in the furniture stores that he became affectionately known as "Uncle Bill." On one occasion, Conrad was heard to say to William, "Will, you just have to get something for us to do in the Shipping Department." The next day William telephoned from Toronto with a large order for basswood-topped kitchen tables to be shipped at once.

Except for one unfortunate occasion when about ten employees were discharged, there were no other layoffs in the factory. Hours of work, however, were severely limited. They were reduced to as short as 8:30 am to 12 noon and

Kitchen tables, shown in assorted sizes, as advertised in the Krug Bros. 1930 catalogue #44. The price list shows the smallest table (2′6″) at $3.10, up to $5.25 for the 6′ table.

KITCHEN TABLES WITH DRAWER
Natural or Golden.
Hardwood Rims and Legs.
Basswood Top, White.
Shipped K.D.
2½ ft. Top, 24x30 inches;
3 ft. Top, 26x36 inches.
3½ ft. Top, 27x42 inches.
4 ft. Top, 28x48 inches.
5 ft. Top, 29x60 inches.
6 ft. Top, 32x72 inches.

1 pm to 4 pm — with a four-day workweek of Monday to Thursday. The regular hours would have been from 7 am to 12 noon and from 1 pm to 6 in the evening, five days a week. This shift in the work schedule came at a time when the European jackrabbit, after having reached this part of Ontario about 1927, had peaked in numbers. Many of the employees supplemented their meat supply at home by going on rabbit drives on their days off.

In order to keep the business going, prices of furniture were severely slashed. Wages and costs of raw materials and other supplies also dropped, easing the situation somewhat. The bottom fell out of the lumber market as the following example illustrates. In 1933, a large block of three-inch-thick hard maple came up for sale at the Minnes Bros. sawmill at Markdale. Before the Depression began in 1929, Minnes Bros. had been offered and had rejected $90 per 1000 board feet for this block. John, Conrad and Christian were taken to Markdale to see this lumber as it could have been used by resawing it. It was decided not to purchase the stock, as it would have meant closing the Chesley sawmill and putting additional employees out of work. This block of hard maple was eventually sold at around $12 per 1000 board feet.

While on his business calls in Toronto, William Krug often called on William Mitchell of "Mitchell & McGill," office furniture specialists, where he occasionally received orders for some special office tables. In 1931, William Krug and William Mitchell got together on a line of oak office desks that helped to pull the business through the bad years. As long as these desks were made for Mitchell & McGill and their successors, Mitchell Houghton Ltd., they were known as the "1931 line of desks." Altogether there were seven different desks in this line, which continued to be manufactured until the early 1959s. This desk line was discontinued when Mitchell Houghton Ltd. fell into financial difficulties. In all, over 37,000 desks were made.

As an aid in keeping the sawmill operating, the prime grade of maple lumber was selected out and shipped through Robt. Bury & Co. Ltd. of Toronto for export to England. A select grade of three-inch-thick elm was also sawn for sale to factories manufacturing hockey sticks. At that time sticks were made of one piece which required three-inch thick lumber.

Wages dropped to very low rates during these years, part of the battle for survival among manufacturers. Starting wages for the boys who did odd jobs dropped to as low as 10 cents per hour and, for men, down to 20 cents. Top wages were about 50 cents per hour. At the time there were no unemployment benefits other than going on relief. Most employees appreciated having work, and every attempt was made to give as steady employment as possible.

The Krug Bros. office staff in the early 1930s. From left to right: Edna Minke, Helen Weick (her father, Jake Weick was foreman in break-out section of the plant), Bert Gillies and William Krug.

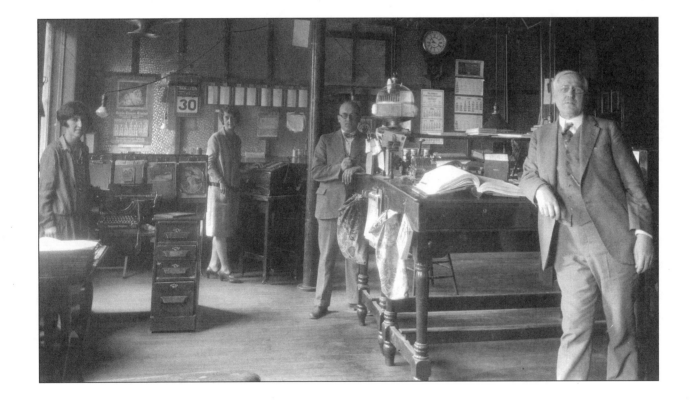

One unsuccessful attempt was made by union people to sign up the factory workers. Furniture factory employees from Owen Sound and Hanover, who had lost their jobs because of cutbacks, arrived as a group at the factory one day. Their leader had checked into the town hotel beforehand. There was much milling about and shouting directed toward the Krug employees. A townsman, who wanted to get closer to the action, drove his team and wagon loaded with heavy gravel to the factory door. The unruly crowd helped themselves to this ready supply of ammunition and began throwing rocks through the windows. During this time all the employees remained inside the factory. The crowd eventually dispersed and the next day the Krug workers voluntarily marched to the town hall to be sworn in as deputies.

Partly because of low wages in the furniture industry, the Ontario government introduced the Industrial Standards Act. If the majority of employees and employers in an industry agreed on certain conditions, including minimum rates and maximum hours of work, the province would enforce these conditions on the whole industry. This helped to end stories of low rates being paid by competitors and brought some control over the competition to lower rates in the industry. The first minimum rate of pay for men was consequently set at 28 cents per hour.

Gradually, especially after 1935, business improved and the factory re-established normal working hours again. The excessive inventory was reduced to normal. With the advent of the Second World War in 1939 and the consequent shortage of labour in a non-essential industry, the warehouse was almost empty by 1943.

Top: The Machine Department at Krug Bros., with the "shaper" machine with knives. This machine created mouldings, made grooves and other decorative touches for furniture. The pipe carried off the dust to the "Cyclone."

Another view of the machine room in the early 1930s. Bert Eby is on the right at the "boring" machine. His son Clifford worked in the veneer department.

Bottom: The Assembly Department, a further stage in the creation of fine furniture.

Note the pile of tabletops to the left in the Sanding Department on the second floor of the factory. The steam pipes running across the ceiling heated the building. During the Depression, daily work hours were shortened in order to maintain as many employees as possible.

Conrad Krug, shown to the extreme left, was in charge of the Shipping Department.

Top, left page:
Harry Moss, the foreman, is leaning against the chair in the Upholstery Room. The chair in the foreground has turned front legs and shaped armrest popular in the 1930s.

Workers in the Finishing Department. The man with the peaked cap, Ernie Durie, is applying a filler to the 1930s-style sideboard.

Bottom, left page:
All the furniture was machine-rubbed, then rubbed by hand to smooth the finish and add lustre.

The final stages of finishing. The pail to the right would have contained a "filler," a paste which was brushed on by hand against the grain of porous woods such as oak, walnut and butternut. Later it was sprayed on, then rubbed off against the grain. This would have been followed by the application of a sealer and varnish.

CHAPTER 11

Later Designs in Furniture

During the 1930s, taste in furniture shifted and the so-called "modern" designs became popular. Many of these were quite plain, with very few carvings and were mostly made with veneer. The use of angle-matched and butt-walnut veneer faces softened the harshness. At the same time, the older-styled, more conventional furniture was decorated using overlays and some spindle carvings. As walnut-finish colour was popular, both solid walnut and those woods which would take a good walnut colour — in combination with the walnut veneer — were used. Walnut veneer was mostly from American black walnut but, during part of this period, the wood known as "oriental wood" or "oriental walnut" from Australia, was used extensively as it could be laid in at a lower price than American walnut.

In the mid-1930s, a modern design developed on case goods became known as the "waterfall." At first this was made with a solid shaped-wood moulding on the front edge of the top. Later, this solid waterfall changed to one in veneer. The face veneer ran from back to front on the tops of the pieces. This could be accomplished in various ways, but the Krug staff worked out their own "waterfall" construction, which proved completely satisfactory. The "waterfall" design became obsolete in the late 1940s.

Soft maple cores were used. At the proper distance from the top edge of the core, two light saw-cuts were scored on the face side of the core, two inches apart. The space between these saw cuts was coated with shellac. A five-ply panel was laid up in the conventional manner except that the face was laid at right angles to the core. The face crossbanding was laid in the same direction as the core. The area that was coated with shellac would not allow the glue to make a bond. After the glued-up panel was trimmed to its proper finished size, two 45-degree angle cuts were made from the underside of the panel so that they just touched the two scored cuts on the face of the core. The 2-inch core between the scoring was next removed. With a little moistening on the face, the top took the required curve in a jig especially made for the purpose. The rounded filler block made of basswood or poplar was then glued in and fastened with nails or screws. There were other methods of getting the "waterfall" effect but, by later observation of these pieces at used furniture markets and sales, it became apparent that the Krug method was superior.

Mention has been made earlier of the sales resistance that had developed towards elm

No. 1610—CHESTERFIELD
Depth 36 inches.   Width 83 inches.   Seat, 24x64 inches.

furniture in the early 1930s. After World War II, however, with a different homeowner now in the market, this sales resistance largely disappeared. Elm lines were again developed, using elm for face woods in both solids and veneers. The solid elm lines proved to be the most popular but had to be dropped in the 1970s when the Dutch elm disease destroyed most of the elm trees in this area.

During the 1920s and 1930s, most of the dining room suites were made with the construction of the buffet and china cabinet having turned, band-sawn or shaped legs of

An upholstered Chesterfield Suite featuring reversible cushions and a spring edge and available in either a mohair covering or tapestry. According to the 1930 price list, the chesterfield in mohair was sold for $69.50.

This Dining Room Suite shown in the 1940 Krug catalogue is described as an all-walnut suite with waterfall fronts.

A 1940 Bedroom Suite described as a combination walnut suite in a waterfall design.

about 18 inches. The suite would consist of nine pieces — buffet, china cabinet, extension table, one armchair and five side chairs. In the 1940s, the credenza-style buffet and china cabinet gained in popularity. Later, a hutch was developed and the china cabinet was dropped. The present-day dining room suite usually consists of a credenza-style buffet, hutch, extension table and four or six chairs.

In bedroom furniture, the vanity dresser virtually disappeared in the late 1930s so that a standard suite consisted of a single dresser, a chest of drawers, a 4 feet 6 inches bed and one or two bedside tables. By 1950, the single dresser was replaced with a double dresser that later gave way to the triple dresser of today.

In the 1950s, bookcase head-ends of beds became popular. While these were in style, the demand for bedside or night tables dropped. However, after about ten years, panel head-ends

This solid plain oak Dining Room Suite, also from the 1940 catalogue, features a refectory style table.

and night tables regained popularity and bookcase head-ends disappeared from the line. In recent years, there is some demand again for the vanity dresser, so one was reintroduced in the 1980s with the #2336 suite.

In the late 1930s, an "Early American" bedroom suite in maple was introduced. This design had become popular in the United States and furniture stores in the American border areas of Essex County and the Niagara region began asking for it. In the 1950s, dining room pieces were added and later, living room furniture and tables. As the demand for this style grew, additional pieces in maple and cherry were introduced. By the 1980s, this style became Krug's main line of furniture. In 1986, about 75% of the factory's production was of the Early American style.

Following World War II, the first new design in dining room furniture was seen in the Duncan Fyfe design, originally drawn up by Ward Hoffman, a freelance furniture designer

The solid elm bedroom suite, advertised in the 1966 Krug catalogue, is described as being constructed from the finest elm grown in the Saugeen watershed and particularly selected for its soft texture and figured grain. The bookcase bed only was listed at $88.00.

from Toronto. This suite was made of walnut or mahogany veneer, combined with local hardwoods. Many factory changes and additions were made to this line as the style was carried on with catalogues featuring designs #3222 and #3244. The style proved to be a steady sales producer for close to 50 years.

Household desks made during this time were of either the secretary-style or the flattop, kneehole design. In 1980, a numbered lot of 50 "Davenport" desks was manufactured. The design was patterned after an antique desk imported from England. This desk proved so popular that, on the company's centennial in 1986, Krug Bros. & Co. manufactured a further 100 numbered desks in solid cherry in the same style, with a few modifications. This desk again proved popular and will, no doubt, be a collectors' item some day.

The standard finish for this solid elm dining room suite is given as "amber," but other finishes (walnut, tavern brown or mahogany) were available on request. The China Cabinet with its glass sliding doors was listed as $138.00 in the September 15, 1966, suggested retail price list.

The 1966 Krug catalogue describes this double dresser as having solid tops of "black cherry... oxbow and swell drawer fronts... hardware of authentic provincial design in brass, especially tailored for this suite." The suggested retail price is $288.00.

The Valencia Bedroom Suite, also in the 1966 catalogue, features a triple dresser. The listed price of $304.00 included the mirror.

2306-1 — Double Dresser
Top — 52″ x 18″. Height 32½″ to 65¾″
Toilet — 43½″ x 31½″
Six Drawers

2306-2 — Chest of Drawers
Top — 32″ x 18″. Height 42″
Four Drawers

2306-3 — Poster Bed
Width — 3′3″ and 4′6″
Height — 61¾″

2306-5 — Night Tabl
Top — 17½″ x 14¾
Height — 25″

No. 2306 Suite

The tops, gables and drawer fronts of this bedroom suite are described as being of solid cherry wood obtained
from trees grown on the high land of the Saugeen watershed, with the bed of solid cherry construction. The catalogue stipulates that
" The skilled craftsmanship and quality materials characteristic of Krug furniture since 1886 are to be found throughout this suite."

The Saugeen Rock Maple Dinette Suite, as featured by Krug Bros. in the looseleaf catalogue of the mid-1970s.

A Step Table, also made from solid rock maple "selected from the best maple found in the limestone country of Bruce and Grey counties."

2228-26 — Desk

No. 2228-6

Desk — Top 50" x 20"
Drawers are 23" wide

2228-16 Desk
Top 46 x 20
6 Drawers

3190-4-D Drop Leaf Extension Table has a folding jacknife
leaf, Table fully extended 72". 38 x 24 x 60 x 72".
3190-5 Chair has a saddle shaped seat.

Saugeen Rock Maple

2228-13 BUNK BED
Standard Finish — Acorn
Also available in Colonial, Cinnamon, Harvest, Cherry
Supplied with ladder and one guard rail. Perma-slat safety bedrails supplied with upper Bed.
Width of Bed is 39", the combined height 66".
These Beds can be set up as Twin Beds.

Opposite page:
Three different styles of desks made of rock maple.

A Drop Leaf Extension Table of rock maple shown with matching chair, 1966.

A Living Room or Recreational Room Suite of the Saugeen rock maple, displayed in the 1966 catalogue.

The rock maple Bunk Bed featuring perma-slat safety bedrails for the upper bed, 1966.

The Duncan Fyfe style Dining Room Suite first introduced by Krug Bros. & Co. in the later 1940s.

A photograph of the burled walnut Davenport desks produced in 1980. At the time they were sold at $350.00 apiece. The price today would be well into the thousands.

CHAPTER 12

Social Activities and Celebrations

Over the years, the Krug Bros. Company was very much part of activities in and around Chesley. Factory picnics were a major activity in the early years of the company's history. The earliest of these were held in Victoria Park in Chesley and were noted for being real community affairs. Later, with the coming of the automobile, the fun was moved to the beach at Port Elgin. Factory trucks were fitted up for the transportation of those who did not own cars.

A most popular feature in Chesley was the band. An apt description is found in *Days of Yore–A Pictoral History of* Chesley, published in

1995:

"The Chesley Citizens Band had its beginning in 1887 as the Mechanics Band, organized by John Krug. Talented musicians were induced to come to Chesley with offers of employment in the factories. Some continued with succeeding bands for over 50 years. The band became a favourite entertainment at socials and garden parties. On New Year's Eve the band would serenade at the homes of the town fathers and quite often would be invited in to share in the

festivities....

On the occasion of the company's 50th anniversary, the evening of May 18, 1936, the Chesley town council arranged for a special commemorative meeting at the town hall. Led by the Chesley band, company employees marched as a group to the hall where the townspeople offered their good wishes. The mayor, Dr. E. K. Dawson presided over the affair; the band played with gusto and H.S. Sanderson led the community singing. The manager of the

The 1928 Programme for the Annual Picnic at Victoria Park in Chesley.

In 1898, the band received a grant of $60 per year from the village, provided they played at a concert in the park every week."

The band has an incredible history, maintaining its presence in the Chesley area for well over a hundred years, from 1887 to 2001.

In 1910, when the building along King Street was constructed, an inaugural bazaar was held there. Tea was served and the usual enjoyable activities for children were arranged, such as a fishpond and ducking for apples.

Chesley Chair Co. employees and the first bicycle in Chesley.

local Bank of Commerce, Tom Henry, presented the company with a bouquet of 50 roses. Sam Allen and Jacob Weick, representing the employees, also presented the owners with a basket of roses and snapdragons. Speeches at the event included a few words from Chesley's "grand old man" W.D. Bell. The town's millionaire, he had acquired his wealth by selling timber to Scotland. (Trained as an engineer, he had been active in the building of the Grand Trunk Railway, bringing it as far as Chesley in 1881. As a man of wealth, he became a patron

The Chesley Mechanics Band founded by John Krug in 1887, photo circa 1905. "They played at wakes and weddings and at every fancy ball." Top row (l to r): Jim Taylor, William Heiserman, George Jarvis; second row from top: William Taylor, Conrad Krug, Fred Park, Jack Heimbecker, Sam Wisler, Nelson Yost; middle row: George Haylock, Jack Elder, Frank Persbacher, Frank McGowan, Harry Wisler, Jack Bartlett; Second row from front: Charles Erdman, George Wright, Charles Green, William Lustig; front row: George Brockie, Herbie Fry. Regrettably, the band was discontinued in January of 2001 after an active lifespan of 114 years. The last bandmaster was Larry Lueck, whose father worked for Krug Bros. and was also in the band. Krug Bros offered employment to bandmasters and musicians to entice them to Chesley, thus maintaining the high quality of performance. During WWI, they were a regimental band. Over the years, the band won many prizes.

The spring fed swimming hole, North Saugeen River, Chesley, Ontario.

employees and their families. Open house continued the next day for the people of Chesley. The wives of W.P. Krug, Stanley Krug and A. R. Siegrist served lunch to the many who attended. A draw for a coffee table was won by one of the employees, Wray Walpole.

And the celebrations continued. In May 1971, on the occasion of the company's 85th anniversary, Mayor Joe Zang presented a clock to the management, bearing the inscription:

To Krug Bros. Furniture
On their 85th year of community service
Town of Chesley

In 1980, when Chesley celebrated its centennial, Miss Risa Clark, who was employed in the company office, was selected to represent the company in the Miss Chesley contest and was the runner-up to the winner.

On the occasion of the 100th anniversary of the company in 1986, major news stories were carried in the media and a celebratory dinner was held at the recreation centre for the employees and their families. The town of Chesley erected a stone monument in front of the factory, which stood on King Street until the summer of 2001. Mason, Ken Warminton, built the plinth with multi-coloured stones gathered

and a preservationist of the town's heritage.) The company was presented with a 50th anniversary marble plaque. The six owners were each given a gold-headed cane.

Twenty-five years later, in 1961, the Krug company's 75th anniversary was celebrated with a special "Open Night" at the showroom for the

1886 **1936**

CIVIC DEMONSTRATION
in Town Hall, Chesley

MONDAY, MAY 18
1936

at 7.30 p.m.

Commemorating the

50th Anniversary
OF THE

Furniture Industry
in Chesley

You Are Welcome!

GOD SAVE THE KING!

A poster announces the forthcoming anniversary celebrations and invites participation from the public.

The crowds gather on Main Street to celebrate the 50th Anniversary of the Krug Bros. Company — 1886 to 1936. Note the white-haired founders standing on an elevated podium to the rear of centre, with the town band, the Mechanics Band, positioned in front. To the left front, the town policeman, Robert Laverty, known locally as "Fleetfoot," is standing near a group of children.

A Century of Excellence: Krug Bros. & Co. Furniture Manufacturers

and split by William Pattison. The plaque, carved by Thomas Soper, was unveiled by Mayor William McClure and local members of the provincial and federal governments made speeches.

It was a bittersweet moment for Howard and Bruce Krug, who were in possession of the sure knowledge that the factory was entering its last days.

The founders of the Krug Bros. & Co. of Chesley gather to celebrate the 50th Anniversary of their company. From left to right: George Krug, Conrad Krug, Henry Ankemann, William Krug, John Krug and Christian Krug, May 1936.

A photograph of the marble plaque presented to the Krug Company on the occasion of its 50th Anniversary in 1936. The plaque is on the wall of the office building now in the process of being demolished.

Howard and Bruce Krug at the unveiling of the commemorative plaque on a cairn celebrating the 100th year anniversary of the Krug Bros. furniture factory in 1986. The cairn will be moved to the site of the original factory on the side of the river. It will sit on Krug Bros. land, which will become Krug Park, donated to the town of Chesley.

CHAPTER 13

Stories For the Retelling

Christmas is often a time of remembering events from previous Christmases. While the founders of the company were still alive, they liked to tell about their first Christmas in Chesley. That Christmas Eve they had received an order for a couch with a special covering. The customer wanted it delivered the next day! The only way to achieve this was to remove the cover from a couch, which was already upholstered, and replace it with the specially ordered covering. Unwilling to lose the order and anxious to please their customer, they went back to work on Christmas day and had the couch ready for delivery by 5 pm that afternoon.

In the early years, when Krug Bros. had a retail store combined with a funeral furniture business, John Krug was given the responsibility of transporting a corpse in a coffin to the cemetery on an open sleigh. On rounding a curve where the snow had drifted badly, the coffin and its occupant slid off the sleigh onto the road — much to John's consternation. Loading it back on to the sleigh, he continued on his way.

In 1896, R. Maxwell of the town line between Sullivan and Elderslie townships delivered seven logs from one pine tree with a total footage of 4,020 feet.

Before the time when the factory was completely serviced for indoor plumbing, an outhouse strategically placed in the yard was used occasionally. One time, when an employee had entered the little building, a great gust of wind toppled it over forward, with the door flat to the ground — of course.

Menno Kaufman, who was the Krug boys' teacher in southeast Hope Township, Perth County in the 1870s, was later established as notary public, conveyancer and insurance agent at Elmwood, not far from the Chesley factory. In 1899, he gave up his business and went on the road for Krug Bros. in southwestern Ontario. He continued in this job until sometime in the 1930s. Travelling in those days was by railway and, when that was not possible, by stagecoach.

Back in the days before the automobile, residents had driving horses. Christian and Conrad Krug were no exception. Each had a pretty, grey driver; sometimes the two were driven together as a team. At the time of the Relief of Ladysmith (the English recaptured Ladysmith which had been besieged by Boer forces during the Boer War of 1899-1902), Chesley organized a big celebration. Conrad took the team out for the parade but with all the commotion of fireworks and shouting, the

horses were frightened and ran away. One of the greys was killed when it ran into a post.

W.P. Krug, son of John, was a keen horticulturist and cultivated a flowerbed along the office wall. One Saturday afternoon, when he was working in this garden in his overalls, some people drove up and expressed a desire to visit the showroom. He willingly obliged them and was much amused when, upon leaving, they

William Krug driving the family's much-loved ponies hitched to a cart in Chesley.

offered to tip him, the gardener.

In April 1924, when the remaining four-storey building on the north side of the river took fire, Tom Bremner was the fire chief and Bob Kidd was the policeman. The firemen were doing everything they could to fight the blaze. Tom was directing the water from his hose onto the fire. Bob thought he should be doing the job differently and didn't hesitate to tell Tom so. Much to the amusement of the large crowd that had gathered at the site Tom, in exasperation, turned his hose on the offending policeman.

Patriotism was strong amongst Canadians during Queen Victoria's reign. When Victoria died in 1901, many corporations brought out some form of postal mourning as a tribute. Krug Bros. had a mailing envelope manufactured with a black band around the stamp.

In 1928, the town of Chesley was amazed but pleased to welcome home, Joost van Os, a former employee of Krug Bros. Van Os was thought to have been killed in action during WWI. His name had been duly engraved on a town memorial among those who had lost their lives. Evidently, van Os who had suffered amnesia after the war found himself working as a chauffeur in London, England. When a blow on the head during an altercation restored his memory, he resolved to return to Canada and his old job at the Chesley factory. When he arrived back in town it was to the utter astonishment of the townspeople — a veritable ghost from the past.

In the early to mid-1980s, several contracts for furniture were received from the External Affairs Department in Ottawa. In 1987, on a trip to Africa, Rev. Crossley Krug, Howard and Bruce Krug's older brother, was amazed to see several pieces of Krug furniture in a home in Harrare, Zambia. It would be interesting to know the global reach of Krug furniture.

CHAPTER 14

Consolidation of the Furniture Manufacturing Industry

Towards the end of the 19th century, a move developed to consolidate the furniture manufacturing industry in Canada, which at that time was based mainly in Western Ontario. In 1898, a proposal was offered to organize the Consolidated Furniture Manufacturing Co. Ltd. with a capital of $3,000,000. The following Ontario based companies, as shown below, were listed for the proposed plan:

The American Rattan Co. Ltd.	Walkerton	The Knechtel Furniture Company	Hanover
The Anthes Manufacturing Co.	Berlin	George McLagan	Stratford
Thomas Bell and Son	Wingham	Schaefer, Killer and Company	Waterloo
Broadfoot and Box Furniture Co.	Seaforth	Siemon and Bros. Manfg. Co.	Wiarton
Burr Bros.	Guelph	The Simpson Company Ltd.	Berlin
Button and Fessant	Wingham	Snyder Roos and Co.	Waterloo
Lewis Hahn	New Hamburg	Watson and Malcolm	Kincardine
D. Hibner and Company	Berlin	Zoellner and Co.	Mount Forest
The Hill Chair Co.	Wiarton	The Furniture Manufacturers Exporting Co.	Berlin, Ontario & London, England
The Hobbs Manufacturing Company	London		
H. Krug	Berlin		
Krug Bros. and Co.	Chesley		

This proposed plan of organization would place the management of the Company in the hands of experienced manufacturers identified, but does not specify any details.

The complete text of this early proposal intended for the Manufacturers' Perusal, is shown in Appendix III. It is not known how far this proposed plan proceeded, but it evidently got things rolling, because in 1900 another proposal was made for organizing the British American Furniture Company Limited with a share capital of $3,000,000. Appendix IV shows an application form for both preferred and common stock in this company. Along with the 21 proposed participating companies in this suggested consolidation were three additional companies: James Young, Wiarton; Joe Orr and Sons, Stratford; and the Union Furniture Co., of Wingham.

The capital stock of the company was to consist of 20,000 preferred shares and 10,000 common shares. Provisional directors were J.R. Shaw and J.L. Tangher of Toronto, W. Hobbs and T.S. Hobbs of London and W.M. Shaw of Walkerton. In a news item in the *Times* of April 6, 1900, mention is made again of this company being organized but the list of names has shrunk to 22 with D. Hibner and Co., H. Krug and George McLagan being deleted and the Chesley Chair Co. Ltd. being added. Production of the amalgamating plants was reported as showing a constantly increasing volume that reached the sum of $1,139,147.00 in 1899.

From the newly proposed company, the following 23 persons consented to act as directors: J.S. and Daniel Knechtel, Hanover; Simon Merner and J.S. Anthes, Berlin; Andrew Malcolm, Kincardine; Henry Cargill, Cargill; R.E. Truax, Walkerton; Thomas Bell and William Betton, Wingham; John H. Broadfoot, Seaforth; Myron W. Burr, Guelph; Lewis Hahn, New Hamburg; Christian Hill and J.C. Siemon, Wiarton; William Krug and John Krug, Chesley; Joseph Orr, Stratford; Henry Schaeffer, Waterloo; E.R. Zoellner, Mount Forest; F.E. Coombe, Liverpool, England; T.S. Hobbs and J.R. Shaw, Toronto; and W.R. Hobbs, London, Ontario. This was an impressive list of those people who were leaders in the furniture and related industries at that time. It offered a deep pool of talent from which to draw up a board of directors.

In November 1900, a suggested prospectus under the new name of the Canada Furniture Manufacturers Limited was issued, see Appendix III for more detailed information. It would be incorporated under the Companies Act of Great Britain with 400,000 preferred shares and 200,000 common shares. All of the common shares and 100,000 of the preferred shares were to be used in the part payment of the various acquisitions. The directors of this company were to be Thomas Gillespie, Nathaniel Burch and Harrison Watson of London, England and W. Hobbs of London, Ontario. The Board of Management in Canada was to be Simon Snyder, President of the Canadian Furniture Manufacturers Exporting Co.; Thomas Bell, President of the Canadian Furniture Manufacturers' Association; Daniel Knechtel, President of the Daniel Knechtel Furniture Co., Andrew Malcolm MPP, furniture manufacturer and William Krug of Krug Bros. & Co. It was at this time that D. Hibner, H. Krug, George McLagan and James Young dropped out of the picture.

It looked as though matters were moving ahead but, beneath the surface, things were not so rosy. Mr. J.R. Shaw of Smellie and Shaw, Barristers & Solicitors in Toronto was doing the organizational work in Canada. Evidently, there was some doubt in the minds of the Krugs as to their place in the new organization. A letter from Mr. Shaw suggested that William would take charge of Burr Bros. at Guelph, Conrad would be in charge of lumber purchasing and Christian, along with the Krug Company bookkeeper, would run the Chesley plant.

Chesley, Hanover and Wiarton operations were to be lumped together for sales purposes. John Krug's name was not mentioned because he was manager of the Chesley Chair Co. Ltd. at this time. The option price for the Krug properties was set at $76,582.15.

Mr. Shaw complained about the slowness of the companies in signing the agreements and sending in photographs of their plants for a full page advertisement he had planned for the *Globe & Mail* edition for Saturday, December 16, 1899 — the same date on which the prospectus was to be issued. As the proposed prospectus did not appear until about a year later, there must have been many obstacles to overcome. A letter from J.R. Shaw to William Krug, dated November 22, 1900, reveals that difficulties were being experienced in raising the funds required from the various Canadian principals. Mr. Shaw pleaded for Krug Bros. to underwrite more of the stock. His view was that the Krug Co. underwriting of $25,000 should be raised by another $12,500.

The amalgamation of the furniture factories eventually took place but on a considerably smaller scale than originally planned. The two Chesley companies, Krug Bros. and the Chesley Chair Co. Ltd., dropped out of the scheme. Information given to Howard

A copy of the advertisement showing photographs of 29 furniture manufacturing plants to be acquired by the Canada Furniture Manufacturers, Limited, planned for publication in the *Globe & Mail*.

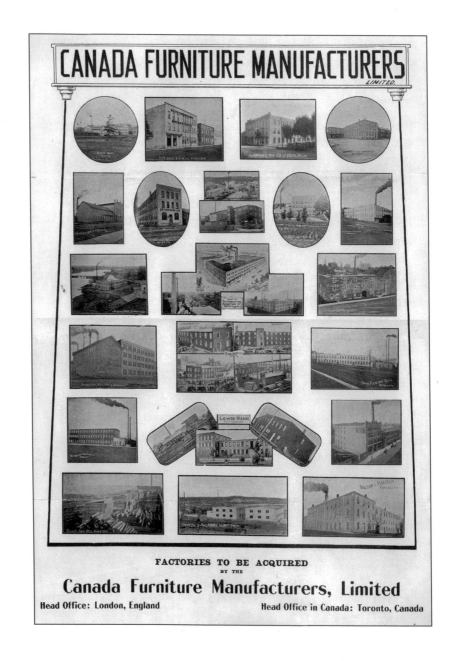

Conrad, Christian, John and William Krug in 1925. The photo was taken by a photographer, George Frehr, employed by Krug Bros. during the Depression.

Krug by his father, Christian, was that the decision to withdraw was influenced by the fact that Krug had a large stock of lumber at the time and wanted cash for it. Promoters of the amalgamation insisted that the lumber be paid for with additional shares in the Canada Furniture Co. but this was not acceptable.

The Krug partners later felt they had made the right decision. Their business continued, after all, for another eighty years — fruitful years in terms of product output and the steady employment of many of Chesley's citizens.

CHAPTER 15

The Concluding Years

The peak years of the Krug factory were from its inception in 1886 till WWI, from the end of that war until the Great Depression, and from 1939 until the advent of the Bruce nuclear facility at Point Douglas near Kincardine in Bruce County in the late 1960s.

Point Douglas drained off employees from businesses throughout a large area in Bruce and Grey counties — and from even further afield. As many as 8,000 people were hired over a period of seventeen years. Wages offered at Point Douglas were considerably higher than the Krug brothers could offer and working conditions, mandated by unions, were softer. Young Krug employees made their way to Point Douglas. Krug's older employees were left without jobs at the 1987 factory closing. Other furniture factories suffered the same fate, notably the Knechtel and Peplar works.

The closing of the Krug factory was a very sad moment for Howard and Bruce Krug even though they had seen it coming. It had been their lives' work and that of their father and their uncles. At its peak in the 1950s, the company employed 150 people. By the time it closed in 1987, the roster was diminished to 60. It had been a struggle to keep it open in the last few years. The economy was in recession and interest rates were high. Competition from Asian furniture makers was growing. And Howard himself was in declining health.

Fortunately, there has been a resurgence in the furniture industry in Chesley in the last ten years. Two thriving factories, Crate Designs and Durham Furniture, carry on the Chesley furniture-making tradition. Crate Designs, with a workforce of about 65 persons, manufactures affordable furniture made of solid yellow pine. The Chesley branch of the Durham Furniture Co. manufactures high-end solid cherry, ash and maple bedroom furniture for the U.S. markets, and employs about 160 people. The furniture tradition in Chesley continues. It was Krug Bros. & Co. that initiated the tradition.

Visual Reminders of the Final Years

Always conscious of the importance of recording their history, Krug Bros. established a photographic record of many who were part of their enterprise in the final years.

These photographs were taken in 1985. Some of them are from the commissioned work of James Siegrist of Chesley, with a few from the Owen Sound *Sun Times*. All are part of the Bruce Krug Collection.

Marion Pavloski.

Wayne Hepburn, foreman of the break-out department.

Roy Farrow, in charge of the finishing department.

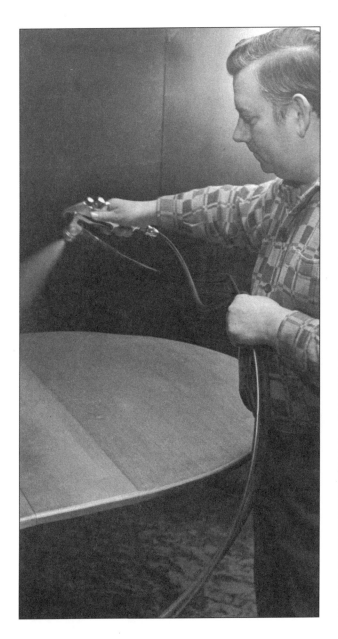

Siegfried Geilenkirchen.

Ken Struke, spray varnishing.

Leslie Streeter, glueing-up manually.

Agnes Byers, at the glueing-up machine.

Alfred Pratt, chairmaker.

Bev Smith, with the cut-off saw.

Bill Krohn at the turning lathe.

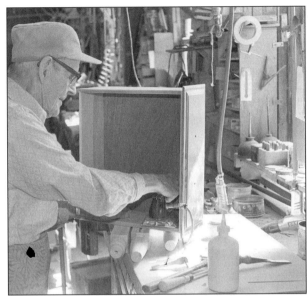

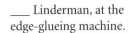 ___ Linderman, at the edge-glueing machine.

Oliver Hallman, foreman, assembling a drawer.

Nancy Schank, in the upholstery department.

Ruth Fry, sanding by hand.

Dan Skrinar,
upholsterer.

John Smith, in the
rubbing department.

John Thomson, head of the shipping department.

Mary Blake, in Krug Bros. office.

Group Photos of Krug Employees, 1950 and 1986

The Krug company was more than just a business venture, it was an integral part of the life of the town of Chesley. Their employees came from Chesley and the surrounding area. The well-being of these dedicated men and women was always of great importance to the Krug Bros.

These surviving industrial photographs capture a past era, a time when the Krug Bros. craftsmanship was unsurpassed. It is Bruce Krug who has kept these memories alive, making every possible effort to identify each employee by name.

Krug Bros. employees and Krug family members photograph taken in May 1950.

First row, seated on planks (l to r):
Percy Lueck,
Wallace Smith,
unknown,
Bob Gaelor,
Charlie Knapp,
Jack Cross,
George Kincaid,
Paul Henkel,
Earl Harron,
Trueman Bruegeman,
Ken Schwartz,
Steve Dustow,
Gordon ?,
Bob Craig.

Second row, seated on chairs (l to r):
Jack Graper,
August Schlacht,
Gerald Valk,
Sam Allen,

Aaron Ankenmann,
Henry Graper,
Howard Krug,
Stan Krug,
Bruce Krug,
William P. Krug,
William Krug,
Emmanuel Schneider,
Margaret Campbell,
Brad Hepburn,
Ephraim Holtzman,
Louis Vanslyke,
Louie Schwinghamer,
Allan Richardson,
Milton Harron,
Sam Hepburn.

Third row, standing (l to r):
Otto Westenberg,
Doug Gaelor,
unknown,
Milton Addison,
Fred Gaelor,
Wes Raeburn,
Willis Trimble,
Walter Gaelor,
Phillip Doer,
Bill Wagner,

Silas Gerrard,
Ruby Lipskie,
Ella Mae Schwarz,
Bill Myles,
Peter Witzke,
Herb Witzke,
Lloyd Steinhoff,
George Ankenmann,
Bill Woods,
unknown,
Ernie Durie,
Jacob Turrel,
Dan McNaughton,
Clint Davidson.

Fourth row, standing (l to r):
Wayne Hepburn,
unknown,
Charlie Barber,
Charlie Crigger,
Jacob Weick,
Lyle Becker,
Bill Arkell,
Alec Becker,
Joe Strba,
Russell Gobert,
Dave Steward,
Adolph Zalman,

unknown,
Oliver Hallman,
Addison Shoemaker,
Bert Eby,
Fred Becker,
August Krigner,
Frank Jefkins,
George Crigger,
Ernest Holmes,
Mike Strba,
Albert Zimmerman,
Herb Brodie.

Fifth row, standing (l to r):
Roy Farrow,
Peter Vandervoort,
Ross Hammond,
John Smith,
Dan Skrinar,
Frank Bilick,
Ken Doer,
Ray Hallman,
unknown,
Bill Stenhoff,
H.A. Smith,
Earl Slomke,
Gottleib Glages,
Richard Wiermeyer,

Jack Johnston,
Ken Sulke,
John Klages,
Lloyd Woods,
Harold Amacher,
Les Streeter,
Mel Schweiger,
Louie Pegelo,
Herman Myers,
Jim Myles,
George Buckland,
Cliff Eby,
George Hepburn.

KRUG BROS. CO. LIMITED.
CHESLEY. ONT. MAY. 1950.

The plaque reads:

TO COMMEMORATE
THE 100TH ANNIVERSARY
OF THE FOUNDING OF
KRUG BROS. CO. LTD.
OPERATED BY
THE KRUG FAMILY
SINCE 1886

PRESENTED BY
THE MUNICIPAL COUNCIL OF
THE TOWN OF CHESLEY
MAY 19, 1986

Group Photos of Krug Employees, 1950 and 1986   163

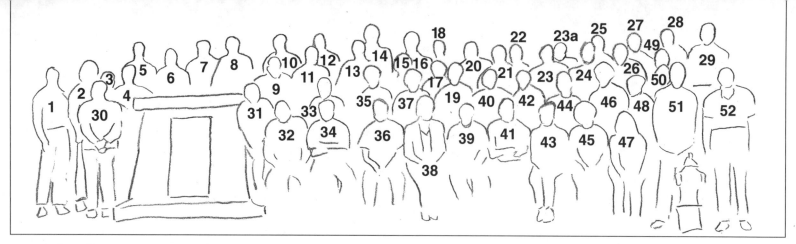

Howard and Bruce Krug join their employees for this 1986 photograph marking the 100th year of Krug Bros. Furniture in Chesley.

The individuals are identified according to the numbers shown on the identification silhouette.

From the left: standing
1. David Johnston,
2. Robin Hepburn,
3. Ruth Fry,
4. Russel Fleischman,
5. Tom Pierce,
6. Ross Hammond,
7. Bev Steward,
8. Jim McFarlane,
9. Hans Bourgeron,
10. Doug Bell,
11. Russel Emke,
12. Bill Jacobs,
13. Lou Albright,
14. Jim Albright,
16. Ed Huber,
17. Elizabeth Robb,
18. Tom Dosworth,
19. Morris Byers,
20. Earl Janke,
21. Vernon Fenton,
22. Ken Pratt,
23. Garry Walpole,
23a. Leith Fenton,
24. Bob Walpole,
25. Herb Brodie,
26. Ken Steinhoff,
27. Connie Klerks,
28. Les Johnston,
29. John Smith,
30. Joyce Hodgson,
31. Earl Beech,
32. Louis Vanslyke,
33. Cathie Lamon,
34. Alfred Pratt,
35. Marion Podelofske,
36. Edgar Schwarz,
37. Marlene Byers,
38. Lynne Collard,
39. Howard Krug,
40. Ray Walpole,
41. Bruce Krug,
42. Dale Emke,
43. Kirsten Lemm,
44. Roger Leblanc,
45. Etta Caroll,
46. Glen Caroll,
47. Marie Caroll,
48. David Zimmerman,
49. Don Struke,
50. Steve Schanke,
51. unknown,
52. Wayne Hepburn.

This photograph was taken on the occasion of Krug Bros. 100th anniversary. Bruce and Howard Krug pose with these formerly retired employees who returned for the celebration.

Front row (l to r): Oliver Hallman, Herman Myers, Harvey Sulkye, Percy Lueck, Wilfred Cotter, Bob Wagner.

Middle row (l to r): Jim Thompson, Albert Zimmerman, Leslie Streeter, Frank Bilick, Joe Strba, Howard Krug.

Back row (l to r): Bruce Krug, Frank Garrett, Cecil Keith, Roy Farrow, Bill Krohn, Anson Fry, Milton Addison.

Furniture Manufacturing Consolidation

The following text is a copy of an original
memo sent to the furniture manufacturing
companies for their perusal, circa 1898.

FURNITURE CONSOLIDATION

MEMO OF PROPOSED PLAN OF ORGANIZATION (for Manufacturers perusal)

NAME   "The Consolidated Furniture Manufacturing Company, Limited.

COMPRISES

The American Rattan Company, Limited	Walkerton
The Anthes Manfg Company,	Berlin
Thomas Bell & Son,	Wingham
Broadfoot & Box Furniture Company	Seaforth
Burr Bros	Guelph
Button & Fessant,	Wingham
Lewis Hahn	New Hamburg
D. Hibner & Company,	Berlin
The Hill Chair Company	Wiarton
H. Krug	Berlin
Krug Bros & Co	Chesley
The Knechtel Furniture Company	Hanover
George McLagan	Stratford
Schaefer, Killer & Company	Waterloo
Siemon & Bros Manfg Co	Wiarton
Snyder Roos & Co	Waterloo
The Simpson Company, Limited	Berlin
Zoellner & Co	Mount Fore
The Hobbs Manufacturing Company,	London
The Furniture Manufacturers Exporting Co	Berlin Ont Liverpool,

EARNINGS

1898,	$170,000
1899 will reach	$200,000

Estimated savings by consolidation $140,000. Say net earnings $300,000.

Share Capital, $3,000,000
    Divided into 30,000 shares of $100 each, as follows:--
    7% Preference Stock (20,000 shares)$2,000,000
    Common Stock limited as to dividend (10,000 shares) $1,000,00

$-------of the Preference Stock has already been subscribed

by certain of the Manufacturers, and will be allotted to them for cash.

$250,000 of the Preference Stock is reserved in the Treasury of the Company for purposes of acquiring other factories, extending present factories or erecting new ones.

The plant, machinery, tools, stock in trade, fixtures, patent rights, trade marks, trade names, good-will and leaseholds of the above named concern in connection with their said business goes to the New Company, including all the real property of all the said concerns but three, viz, Snyder Roos & Co, The Hobbs Manfg Company, and The Furniture Manufacturers Exporting Company, who are in leasehold premises.

MANAGEMENT

The management of the Company will be in the hands of experienced manufacturers who have been identified with the above concerns.

WORKING CAPITAL

The Company will commence business without any bonded or mortgage debts and with a working capital of in excess of over $750,000, exclusive of the additional capital available from the issue of the preference stock in the Treasury $250,000.

DIVIDENDS (Preferred Stock)

The Preference Shares shall confer the right to a fixed cumulative preferential dividend of seven per centum per annum, accruing from the date of payment by subscribers, to be provided for out of the net earnings of the Company before any dividends are paid upon the Common Stock, and the further right to repayment of capital in priority to the Common Stock, and if the earnings of the Company warrant it, they will further participate with the Common Stock in the earnings of the Comp-

any pro rata after payment of the amount hereinafter stipulat-
ed into a reserve account, and 9% on the Common Stock.

If in any one year, dividends amounting to 7% are not paid on
the Preference Stock, the deficiency shall be a first charge
upon the net earnings of the Company, and shall be paid sub-
sequently before any dividend is paid upon or set apart for
the Common Stock.

Dividends will be payable half yearly, on the 1st day of ----
and --------or such other half yearly dates as the Directors
shall determine.

RESERVE ACCOUNT

The Charter of the Company will provide that, *not less* 25% of the balance
of the net earnings, after payment of the 7% dividend on the
Preference Stock, shall be annually transferred to a Reserve
Account in the books of the Company, the better to secure to
the Preference Shareholders payment of the 7% dividend on
their Preferred stock, and such annual transfers shall be
continued until the amount of such account reaches $500,000
at which sum it is to be maintained, and if it is at any time
drawn upon, it is to be in like manner restored and maintained.

DIVIDEND (Common Stock)

After payment of the said 7% dividend on the Preferred Stock,
and making provision for the said Reserve Account, the balance
of the net earnings shall be ~~applied in payment~~ *not exceeding* of a dividend
on the Common Stock ~~to the extent~~ of 7%. If the amount available exceeds a sum which would be equal to 7% on the Common
Stock, the surplus is available to be divided pro rata between
the Preferred and Common Stock or to further extend or develop
business.

ASSETS

It is proposed that the New Company shall purchase from the

Manufacturers their stock in trade, manufactured and unmanufact
ured which as far as can be estimated amounts to $528,375, 83

The plant &c., as nearly as can be estimated from the figures
in my possession amounts to $827,613.64. Additions to plant
and machinery would raise this to $900,000. Cash capital
$250,000. Total $1,676,375.83.

The Manufacturers will get in cash under the old proposition
for their stock $528,375.83, half the $900,000--$450,000 and
Stock preferred $450,000.

$250,000 of the cash capital has got to be raised, therefore,
$528,375.83, plus $450,000, plus $250,000 would make $1,228,375.83
of cash to be raised, and in order to do this stock would be
placed in the Brokers hands at 95¢ on the dollar by the under
writers. 5% of $1,228,000 would amount to $61,400 which sum
added to the assets would make $1,739,775.83, say $1,750,000
on which amount only interest is to be paid as the other
$250,000 is lying in the Treasury. 7% on $1,750,000 would re
quire $122,500. If our income were, say, $300,000 we deduct
this from the income leaving $178,500. 25% of which is to
be laid aside to Rest Account as above stated. On these
figures this would amount to $44,625, leaving a balance of in
come $133,875 on $1,000,000 Common Stock to be paid 7% this
would take $75,000, leaving $63,875 to be divided between the
Preference and Common, thus enabling the dividend to be raised from 7% on each stock to a little over 9%.

You will see by the plan that the preference Stock is gild
edged, and equal to cash.

Before going to Montreal and asking the Underwriters to under
write the $1,228,000, I want to see if you will not take more
than $450,000 in stock. This amount you have agreed to take.

I believe that we should retain contol of this Company. I believe also in giving the Manufacturers a first chance so that I have proposed to them for every dollar they take over and above half of their plants in Stock that they get a bonus of 25% of Common Stock.

Illustration

If your plants and stock are worth $15,000 of which $5,000 is stock $10,000 factory, I have agreed to give you $5,000 for the stock in cash, $5,000 cash and $5,000 preference for the factory, and this I will do, but if you will take instead the $10,000 in Preferred Stock instead of cash, I will give you $2,500 in Common Stock as a bonus. If $5,000 I will give you $1,250. I want to get as much of this stock as I can, taken up by the Manufacturers. When I go down to Montreal in stead of asking them to underwrite $1,228,000 be able to say that the Manufacturers themselves think so well of thebscheme that instead of taking only one third in cash they are tak- ing a much larger proportion, and I only want your assistance for a much lesser amount than I first expected, viz $--------

Canadian Furniture Trade 1894

APPENDIX V

Form for Application For Stock in the British American Furniture Company, Limited

British American Furniture Company, Limited.

HEAD OFFICE, - TORONTO.

SHARE CAPITAL, - - - - - - - $3,000,000
DIVIDED INTO 30,000 SHARES OF $100.00 EACH, AS FOLLOWS:
7 per cent. Preference "Cumulative" Stock (20,000 Shares) - $2,000,000
Common Stock (10,000 shares) - - - - - - $1,000,000

To MESSRS. R. WILSON-SMITH, MELDRUM & CO.,
Financial Agents, Montreal.

GENTLEMEN,—
I hereby apply to the said Company for and agree to take.......................................shares of $100 each at par of the Preference Stock of the **British American Furniture Company, Limited**, and I beg to hand you herewith
....Dollars ($..................) being 10% of the amount of this subscription.

I agree to pay the balance as follows:

25% on 10th May, 1900; 25% on 10th June, 1900; and 40% on 10th July, 1900. And I agree to take such less number of shares on this subscription as may be allotted to me by the said Company.

Dated at..........................this................day of...........................1900.

Witness:

Name (in full)...

Address...

NOTE.—Payments to be made payable to the order of The Merchants Bank of Canada.

Furniture Manufacturing Companies in 1942, 1987 and 2001

FURNITURE MANUFACTURING COMPANIES IN 1942*

BRUCE COUNTY

Chesley Manufacturing Co.	Chesley
Chesley Chair Co. Ltd.	Chesley
Krug Bros. Co. Ltd.	Chesley
Coombe Furniture Co. Ltd.	Kincardine
Andrew Malcolm Furniture Co. Ltd.	Kincardine
Filton Parker Co. Ltd.	Southampton
Hepworth Furniture Co. Ltd.	Southampton
M.M. Homel	Mildmay
Wiarton Furniture Co. Ltd.	Wiarton
Lucknow Table Co. Ltd.	Lucknow
Bogden and Gross Co. Ltd.	Walkerton

GREY COUNTY

Ball Furniture Co. Ltd.	Hanover
Keener Up. Co.	Hanover
Knechtel Kitchen Kabinet Ltd.	Hanover
Peppler Bros. Co. Ltd.	Hanover
Spiez Furniture Co. Ltd.	Hanover
National Table Co. Ltd.	Hanover
North American Bent Chair Co. Ltd.	Hanover
Harris Furniture Co. Ltd.	Hanover
Durham Furniture Co. Ltd.	Durham
Idle (Thos.) Co.	Thornbury
Meaford Furniture Co. Ltd.	Meaford

HURON COUNTY
John Boshart and Sons   Seaforth
Fry and Blackhall Ltd.   Wingham

PERTH COUNTY
Farquharson-Gifford Co. Ltd.   Stratford
Imperial Rattan Co. Ltd.   Stratford
Kroehler Mftg. Co. Ltd.   Stratford
Preston-Noelling Ltd.   Stratford
Stratford Chair Co. Ltd.   Stratford
Wellington Novelties   Stratford
Andrew Malcolm Furniture Co. Ltd.   Listowel
Honderich Furniture Co. Ltd.   Listowel

FURNITURE MANUFACTURING COMPANIES IN 1987*

GREY COUNTY
Sklar Peppler   Hanover
Kroehler   Durham

BRUCE COUNTY
Heirloom of Canada   Chesley
Krug Bros. Co. Ltd.   Chesley
Bogden and Gross   Walkerton

* Information taken from thesis of W.H. Draper.

FURNITURE MANUFACTURING COMPANIES IN 2001**

BRUCE COUNTY
Crate Designs Ltd.   Chesley
Durham Furniture Inc.   Chesley
Bogden & Gross   Walkerton

GREY COUNTY
West Furniture Co. Inc.   Hanover
Durham Furniture Inc.   Durham

** Information from Bruce Krug.

Index

ABOUT THE AUTHOR

ABOUT THE EDITOR

Howard Krug's long life (1904-1997) was characterized by singleness of purpose. Except for his years at the University of Toronto, where he earned a degree in Forestry, he lived and worked in Chesley, Ontario. Here, he learned the craft and business of furniture-making in the family firm of Krug Bros. As a young man he worked through every department of the business in the traditional manner of apprenticeship — eventually succeeding his father as the chairman. For many years he also participated in the wider work of the Ontario Furniture Makers' Association.

Howard Krug was an ardent outdoorsman who managed crews mapping out portions of the Bruce Trail. He was an enthusiastic bird bander, a skilled and farsighted woodsman, as well as a boys' club instructor in the arts of outdoor living. A gifted athlete, he particularly enjoyed tennis, curling and skiing.

Ruth Cathcart is the author of *Jacques & Hay— 19th Century Toronto Furniture Makers* and two books on the subject of historic Canadian architecture, *How Firm a Foundation—Historic Houses of Grey County, Ontario* and *The Architecture of a Provincial Society—Houses of Bruce County, Ontario—1850-1900*. As an Albertan transplanted to Ontario in 1970, she encountered the history and artifacts of early Canada which inspired the research which led to writing on the subject of antiques and architecture and the establishment of an antiques business in Toronto. She is now retired and living near Owen Sound, Ontario.